D0841214

KISSINGER'S
GRAND DESIGN

KISSINGER'S
GRAND DESIGN.

G. Warren Nutter

With a foreword by Melvin R. Laird

American Enterprise Institute for Public Policy Research
Washington, D. C.

G. Warren Nutter is Paul Goodloe McIntire professor of economics, University of Virginia, adjunct scholar of the American Enterprise Institute, and former assistant secretary of defense for international security affairs.

ISBN 0-8447-3186-2

Foreign Affairs Study 27, October 1975

Library of Congress Catalog Card No. 75-33509

Printed in the United States of America

CONTENTS

FOREWORD

In the American political system, Congress and the presidency represent coequal branches of government, and both have important roles to play in framing and implementing foreign policy. Our nation cannot long sustain any course of foreign relations not endorsed by both branches and, of course, the citizenry at large. It follows that foreign policy must be shaped by discussion, agreement and public understanding.

There are many dimensions to foreign policy: the long-term structure of relationships, the day-to-day conduct of affairs, the management of crises, the mediation of disputes, the projection of influence, and the assessment of realities. Each demands particular skills; it is not enough to master some and not all.

But the complex of foreign policy actions will assume coherence and purpose only if it conforms to a grand design. In this era of awesome power, we risk destruction and our national survival if we try to muddle through.

What grand design should set the context of our foreign policy? What ultimate objectives should underlie our diplomacy? And how should these be developed and achieved? These issues need discussion, and that is the purpose of this study: to contribute to the competition of ideas in the public policy forum.

Consensus on the broad outlines and underlying assumptions of foreign policy is the goal, and it can be reached only if we are willing to listen to criticism as well as praise. The critique presented in this study by Warren Nutter deserves to be read and considered.

MELVIN R. LAIRD

KISSINGER'S GRAND DESIGN

Prologue

Rapid change is sometimes revealed more by the receding past than by the unfolding present or future. So it is with our foreign policy. Détente has a negative rather than a positive significance: it marks the end of an old order without symbolizing the beginning of a new one. We are naturally led to wonder whether it is the product of drift or design.

There surely was a grand design to containment, the policy now come to an end—a design that was comprehended and, during most of its life, supported by the American public. It grew out of shared experience and came to be formulated by political leaders who in essence were doers, not thinkers. As a people, we recognized the Soviet drive for global hegemony as the dominant menace to a peaceful world order and resolved to contain it—rather late of course, since Soviet power was in no small measure the creature of our own naive and neglectful diplomacy in the years surrounding World War II.

To say that there was a grand design to containment is not to argue that it was right then or suited to all time. Alterations in the worldwide configuration of power over recent years have rendered some of its basic postulates obsolete, while Vietnam demonstrated that the United States will no longer be the lonely grand protector of Western civilization. Some would argue that the entire policy was wrong from the beginning. But all that is quite another matter. The point is that the policy of containment was, until Vietnam, the conse-

I am indebted to Clifford Kiracofe and William Nutter for assistance in research, and to Marie-Christine MacAndrew, Anne Hobbs, and Carolyn Southall for help in preparing the manuscript.

quence of government by discussion and consensus. It was understood and implemented by the public, by Congress, and by every component—elected, appointed, and career—of the executive branch, all in open communication with each other. Those who disagreed knew at least what they disagreed with and about.

We have, it might seem, even more reason to expect the same today. Our foreign policy is shaped by Henry Kissinger, an articulate thinker of extraordinary intellectual gifts and an ardent advocate of conceptual framework first, policy second. He has filled many pages with briefings, interviews, and expositions explaining the rationale behind a multitude of actions. Yet, through it all, one has the eerie sensation of being told only where we have been, not where we are going.

Where, when all is said, are we headed in the domain of foreign affairs? Is there a grand design to our foreign policy? That is the subject of this enquiry, which searches for Kissinger's conceptual framework.

Kissinger's Outlook as a Scholar

The world outlook of Kissinger the scholar is evident in the main body of his academic writings. It changed little in fifteen years and is perhaps nowhere better summarized than in the crisp opening pages and other concise passages of his first book, *A World Restored*, written in 1954 and published three years later.[1] At base lies the conception of peace as a stability of forces within a legitimate international order of comity, custom, and law. The order is legitimate, in Kissinger's lexicon, if its inherent constitutional rules of conduct are respected by all major powers. Unless a stable order is achievable, the quest for peace is bound to be self-defeating. Hence the statesman has the paramount duty of creating and preserving stability.

Peace means settlement of problems through a consensual process, he argued, not absence of international conflicts. When the constitutional order itself comes into issue, nations face a revolutionary situation in which diplomacy can no longer resolve differences. Since the system itself is the object of disagreement, the conflict is ideological and resolvable only through exercise of power. A long-established stable order may fall precisely because the status-quo powers, having become so accustomed to spontaneous conformity, find it hard to take a revolutionary power seriously when it proclaims

---

[1] The passages referred to here and other pertinent quotations from Kissinger's works are given in the appendix to this study.

2

its intention to reshape the world. France under Napoleon was such a revolutionary power, and so was Germany under Bismarck's tutelage and again after Versailles. Today's revolutionary powers are the Soviet Union and the People's Republic of China.

Kissinger was fascinated by the prominent diplomatic figures of revolutionary periods in the nineteenth century, but he studied them to discern the innovative nature of their statecraft and to discover the secret of their personal success in shaping the world, not to memorize concrete patterns of diplomacy that might prove useful today. On the contrary, he has always stressed that the revolutionary situation confronting us is unique in both origin and portent. An explosive environment has come into being: international relations have become global in scope, military power has become polarized while other aspects of power—political, economic, and moral—have been diffused among nations, and the implements of war have become potentially holocaustal. A balance of power in its classical sense has lost meaning because marginal adjustments in power have become impossible: strategic nuclear weapons have eliminated the territorial basis of power and endowed military strength with a cataclysmic dimension that cannot be neutralized by gathering together increments of counterforce through the traditional process of alliance. Within this environment, major powers are joined in an ideological struggle of epic proportions, while an unassimilated third world of emerging nations contemplates which way to jump.

Such a context compels diplomacy to become symbolic if it is to be effective. In a stable world order, power is the handmaiden of diplomacy; in a revolutionary situation, the roles are reversed. Negotiation becomes a means of building a case, striking a pose, stiffening resolve, and forging coalitions, not of settling disputes. Compromise being alien to the nature of a revolutionary power, only a fool will formulate negotiating positions as points of departure for a genuine bargaining process. They should instead be cast as tactical maneuvers designed to demonstrate to onlookers the intransigence and unreasonableness of the revolutionary power, for nothing short of capitulation can reassure it. In these circumstances, the influential diplomat addresses the grandstand, not the negotiating table.

Power must be the ultimate recourse in resisting revolutionary pressures, and therefrom springs the dreadful dilemma of the day: whether to acquiesce to encroachments or to resist them, when resistance carries the risk of annihilation. Crassly put, the dilemma is one of surrender or suicide. Kissinger met it head-on in his second book, *Nuclear Weapons and Foreign Policy*, also published in 1957.

To him the answer was to restore the plausibility of war by shaping a strategy likely to limit warfare to whatever scale fits the magnitude of the threat being repulsed. At first, he argued for a strategy placing reliance on early use of tactical nuclear weapons, but he shortly revised his position [2] by calling for initial recourse to conventional arms. Limited war will be perceived by an aggressor as credible, he argued, only if the threatened powers are visibly prepared to resist with strong conventional forces. There must, at the same time, be both a capability and a likelihood of appropriate resort to nuclear weapons in order to deter an aggressor from practicing nuclear blackmail or recklessly escalating a limited war once engaged. Warfare so contained by both sides will lead to something less than victory or defeat in the conventional sense, but it will deny to the aggressor what he seeks, and that is the objective.

In the face of a determined revolutionary power armed with modern weapons, there is no way of being sure that a limited war will not get out of hand. Some risk is always present of an ultimate cataclysm. But, whereas this is the worst possible result of a well-rounded strategy, it is the only outcome of a single-minded strategy of massive retaliation or assured destruction when deterrence fails and the stakes are high. If the stakes are not quite high enough, the single-minded strategy will lead inevitably to surrender. When defense through limited war becomes plausible, there is a good chance for something better than surrender at the one extreme or annihilation at the other. Conventional warfare is also the only feasible means of holding territory, and it is easier militarily and psychologically to defend ground than to retake it. All things considered, Kissinger therefore viewed a strong conventional posture backed by a credible strategic and tactical nuclear capability as the best hope for deterring the spectrum of alternative strategies open to a revolutionary power: all-out aggression, nibbling tactics, and nuclear blackmail.

What, then, to do? Kissinger saw North Atlantic unity as the key to resistance and resolution of the German question as the key to Atlantic unity. Political cohesion, ultimately through federal union, was seen as requisite for removing doubts about the reliability of the U.S. nuclear deterrent, enabling nuclear weapons to be controlled in common, and preventing nuclear proliferation. Political bonds would become all the more important as an atmosphere of détente developed and consequently weakened the cohesive force provided

---

[2] In "Limited War: Nuclear or Conventional? A Reappraisal," *Daedalus*, Fall 1960, pp. 800-817. This article is reproduced and expanded in *The Necessity for Choice* (New York: Harper and Row, 1961), Chapter 3.

by fear of a common enemy. The best solution would be political integration of the entire Atlantic community; the next best, European federation accompanied by a pooling of French and British nuclear forces. Militarily, the most important single task would be to constitute a formidable local defense by building up the conventional forces of Europe without reducing those of the United States.

European defense, Kissinger argued, was inconceivable without full participation of Germany, politically and militarily. "The ideal situation," he wrote, "would be a Germany strong enough to defend itself but not strong enough to attack, united so that its frustrations do not erupt into conflict and its divisions do not encourage the rivalry of its neighbors, but not so centralized that its discipline and capacity for rapid action evoke countermeasures in self-defense."[3] Granting that unification of Germany within the discernible future was ruled out by the facts of life, Kissinger insisted that the West must nonetheless persist in advocating that it be achieved through self-determination. Unless the onus for thwarting German unification were brought to rest squarely on the Soviet Union, the Federal Republic of Germany could not be expected to place full reliance on membership in the Atlantic community as the best means of furthering its national interests. It would instead be tempted to deal separately with the Soviet Union, thereby initiating a scramble for accommodation or collaboration on the part of other European nations and unraveling the Atlantic alliance. The collapse of NATO's resolve to resist would quickly lead to acquiescence to Soviet power elsewhere, and the struggle would be over by default.

There was no doubt in Kissinger's mind that the cause of European unity required a stern refusal to legitimize East Germany in its Soviet form. Recognition must be linked firmly to the prerequisite of self-determination, since movement toward German unification on any other basis would be self-contradictory. The outcome could only be Soviet hegemony over all of Germany. If self-determination is out of the question, let the Soviet Union bear the onus of preventing it. The policy of the West should then be to isolate East Germany, not to expand relations with it. Similarly, the West should not negotiate away the independence of West Berlin or legitimize the status of East Berlin under the illusion that any permanent agreement with the East on the status of Berlin, no matter how bad, is better than none. Acceding to the Soviet position on Berlin and Eastern Germany would be the beginning of the end. On the other hand, the West should respect the reasonable concerns of Germany's neighbors over

---

[3] *Necessity for Choice*, p. 129.

the potential threat posed by a reunified Germany. Hence the Federal Republic should recognize the Oder-Neisse boundary with Poland and, in exchange for German unification, agree to some international controls over deployment of armed forces in Central Europe.

But, in the absence of a unified Germany, such controls make no sense. In the first place, the problem with the Soviet Union as a revolutionary power is not that it feels threatened by other powers, but that nothing they can do short of capitulation will reassure it. Secondly, NATO forces are already too weak in size, armament, and disposition to provide an adequate sense of security to the Atlantic community, so that any feasible disengagement scheme would merely exaggerate the imbalance of power in favor of the East and further demoralize the West.

Under existing circumstances, the security of Europe against the threat of local aggression could be improved only by a combination of actions and controls on both sides. These would include building up Western forces, reducing Eastern forces, agreeing to ceilings implied by such a realignment, and controlling territorial deployment. This complex of elements would then have to be monitored by an inspection system with tolerable limits of accuracy. The likelihood that such an arrangement could be negotiated seemed remote to Kissinger.

Strategic arms limitation was the one area in which he thought negotiation with Communist states might be fruitful. For any chance of success, however, the West must have the objective of improving security for all parties, and it must not pin all its hopes on a successful outcome and in particular leave the impression that all is lost unless some—any—agreement is reached. In addition, both sides must be aware of the need to adapt controls to changing circumstances. Kissinger's specific proposals, put forth at various times, are of interest today only as objects of historical curiosity. Less dated is his constant insistence that the goal of arms control should be to reduce the risks of surprise attack, accidental war, and proliferation, not to save money on defense budgets; that control of nuclear arms must be coupled with restoration of a balance of conventional forces if security was to be improved in the West in any fundamental sense; and that "effective schemes require careful, detailed dispassionate studies and the willingness to engage in patient, highly technical negotiations." [4]

On the more fundamental issues dividing East and West, Kissinger could not conceive of negotiation, even when skillfully conducted, as accomplishing any lasting settlement by itself. He had nothing but

[4] Ibid., p. 213.

scorn for most Western diplomatic efforts, finding them clumsy and based on a host of false premises: that Soviet feelings of insecurity could be assuaged by Western concessions, that a favorable evolutionary transformation of Soviet society was under way, that détente or relaxation of tensions or peaceful coexistence would be equivalent to peace, that most differences were rooted in misunderstanding on the part of Communist authorities and hence could be resolved through personal diplomacy. Adenauer and de Gaulle alone seem to be the statesmen for whom Kissinger found a soft spot in his heart, in both cases because he admired their realism and creative vision. He was scathing in denunciation of American diplomacy under Eisenhower and Dulles, characterizing it as fatuous, moralistic, and maudlin, though perhaps less so than British diplomacy under Macmillan. He was less unkind to the Kennedy and Johnson administrations without wasting words of praise.

The worst features of diplomacy were, he thought, embodied in the summitry of the fifties and sixties. Such "ambulatory diplomacy," in the absence of a unified program or strategy of the West, merely played into the hands of an intransigent Soviet leadership, which by virtue of its dictatorial powers could distort and manipulate issues at pleasure and thereby demoralize its Western suitors. It was a fundamental mistake to pursue diplomacy on a personal rather than an institutional plane, particularly in the absence of a coherent program encompassing concrete negotiations.

Nor, he said, should détente be sought for its own sake. Despite the fact that the Soviet tactic of turning "peace offensives" on and off has a long history, on the occasion of each new one there are many in the West who want to believe that this time it is real. The wish-thought persists, even though each period of détente has been brought to a halt by Soviet leaders when they could not resist seizing an opportunity to expand Soviet hegemony. Détente is usually a Soviet response to a temporary strain on the Soviet system, never a shift in Soviet objectives. The West can secure lasting benefits from a period of détente only if it takes advantage of Soviet weakness of the moment through a concerted diplomatic program backed by a credible defense posture. Otherwise, the spirit of détente will merely add the final touch to Western disintegration. The Soviet campaigns of peaceful coexistence in the fifties and sixties seemed, in fact, to have been motivated mainly by anticipation that they would demoralize the West.

Underlying the exhortations, criticisms, and prescriptions of Kissinger the scholar is an unmistakable vision of the West in decline.

But far from believing in historical determinism, he conceives a critical role for human will and imagination in shaping the course of events within the constraints forged by facts and circumstances. The great statesman in particular, depending on his strength of will and powers of perception, can mold order out of seeming chaos. His task is to be creative while acquiring domestic support for policies whose wisdom may not be discernible in advance.

In his concept of the ideal statesman, Kissinger comes close to professing a great-man theory of history and advocating an aristocratic cast to government, at least in the area of foreign affairs. In his first book, he describes this philosophy in the following words:

> The statesman is therefore like one of the heroes in classical drama who has had a vision of the future but who cannot validate its "truth." Nations learn only by experience; they "know" only when it is too late to act. But statesmen must act *as if* their intuition were already experience, as if their aspiration were truth. It is for this reason that statesmen often share the fate of prophets, that they are without honour in their own country, that they always have a difficult task in legitimizing their programmes domestically, and that their greatness is usually apparent only in retrospect when their intuition has become experience.[5]

The need for creativity in Western foreign policy is a prevalent and recurrent theme in Kissinger's writings, the implication being that creative policy will be beneficial, though we are not told why. Nor are we told how to identify or recognize the creative statesman in advance of the test of time. The notion of the creative mind assumes a metaphoric and almost mystical air, only slightly dispelled when Kissinger contrasts it with bureaucratic and ideological mentalities.

Bureaucracy, being a mechanism for administering the affairs of government, has the mission of executing policy already determined, and it fulfills that mission, Kissinger notes, by fragmenting responsibilities, transforming tasks into routine procedures, and adjusting behavior to the facts of life. Caution is the watchword since failure in an assigned task is far more likely to carry a penalty than success in an innovative venture is to bring a reward. Bureaucracy breeds dependence on a host of experts, each reigning in his isolated and specialized domain. When, as in the United States, policy making is dominated by the bureaucratic frame of mind, it becomes the captive of history, drifting aimlessly wherever the admixture of objective

---

[5] *A World Restored: Castlereagh, Metternich and Restoration of Peace, 1812-1822* (Boston: Houghton-Mifflin, 1957), p. 329.

forces and bureaucratic vested interests carries it. Each problem is met as it arises, being treated "on its own merits" and pragmatically resolved by some compromise course of action based on the various extreme positions advocated by components of the bureaucracy.

The ideological leader experiences another kind of mental confinement, one imposed by the rigidities of dogma. In our time, the worst examples of domineering ideology are to be found in Communist countries, where leaders have been brought up to believe that the course of history is predestined by objective societal factors, decipherable only through the Marxist-Leninist theory of history. Taken literally, this ideology asserts that the statesman cannot be creative because the course of events results solely from the "correlation of forces" deriving from the dialectic of the class struggle.

The creative statesman is constrained in his thinking by neither routine nor dogma. Indeed, in Kissinger's view, to create is to use history in molding a novel order of things, and not to be used by history. And so he says:

> The issue may therefore turn on a philosophical problem described earlier. The overemphasis on "realism" and the definition of "reality" as being entirely outside the observer may produce a certain passivity and a tendency to adapt to circumstance rather than to master it. It may also produce a gross underestimation of the ability to change, indeed to create, reality. To recapture the ability and the willingness to build our own reality is perhaps our ultimate challenge.[6]

Creativity is, then, an act of will by the great man causing the order of things and the course of events to be materially different from what they otherwise would have been. Why to be different is also to be better is, as already observed, left unexplained.

However vague Kissinger may be about the attributes and benefits of creative statesmanship, he leaves no doubt about his contempt for bureaucracy and his conviction that Western foreign policy, molded bureaucratically, is certain to fail. If the statesman is to meet the challenge of the times, he must surmount the bureaucracy, escape its clutches, and set the directions of foreign policy through other channels altogether.

Kissinger's Outlook as a Public Official

When we leave the academic years and move into the period of public service, it obviously becomes more difficult to follow the evolution

---

[6] *Necessity for Choice*, p. 357.

of Kissinger's world outlook. By nature, official pronouncements are filled with more rationalization than rationale, more slogans than concepts. And then there is the simple question of who was the principal architect of foreign policy those first five years, Nixon or Kissinger. Whatever the answer, a noticeable change in the cast, tone, and content of Kissinger's public utterances occurred once he had assumed the office of secretary of state. It is therefore to documents issued since the fall of 1973 that we shall look to discern the trend of Kissinger's thinking, assuming it is discernible. We shall look in particular to his statement of September 1974 before the Senate Foreign Relations Committee, his most comprehensive profession of political philosophy since becoming a public official.

In Secretary Kissinger's first major address, at the Third Pacem in Terris Conference, he makes a pass at disarming critics while seeming to meditate biographically when he contrasts the roles of critic and policy maker and pleads for mutual understanding. He notes that

> the critic is obliged to stress imperfections in order to challenge assumptions and goad actions. . . . The policy maker must be concerned with the best that can be achieved, not just the best that can be imagined. He has to act in a fog of incomplete knowledge without the information that will be available later to the analyst. He knows—or should know—that he is responsible for the consequences as well as for the benefits of success. He may have to qualify some goals, not because they would be undesirable if reached but because the risks of failure outweigh potential gains. He must often settle for the gradual, much as he might prefer the immediate. He must compromise with others, and this means to some extent compromising with himself.[7]

There is, of course, nothing new in this lesson learned, merely the universal experience that bearing responsibility makes a difference.

That experience may explain some of the profound changes that have taken place in Kissinger's conceptual framework, changes embodied in what has come to be known as the policy of détente. He has implicitly renounced his earlier conviction that only the exercise of power can check Soviet strife with the Western world and that, unless Soviet weakness is exploited, détente will merely hasten Soviet hegemony by demoralizing the West. "Détente is an imperative," he now says. "In a world shadowed by the danger of nuclear holocaust, there is no rational alternative to the pursuit of relaxation of

---

[7] *Department of State Bulletin*, October 29, 1973, p. 527.

tensions."[8] That is, avoidance of the *risk* of war must be the supreme and overriding goal of U.S. policy, almost regardless of cost in other respects.

This attitude stands in stark contrast to the sober warning on the opening page of Kissinger's first book:

> Those ages which in retrospect seem most peaceful were least in search of peace. Those whose quest for it seems unending appear least able to achieve tranquillity. Wherever peace—conceived as the avoidance of war—has been the primary objective of a power or a group of powers, the international system has been at the mercy of the most ruthless member of the international community. Whenever the international order has acknowledged that certain principles could not be compromised even for the sake of peace, stability based on an equilibrium of forces was at least conceivable.[9]

He made the same point in those early years when he noted that "the dilemma of the nuclear period can, therefore, be defined as follows: the enormity of modern weapons makes the thought of war repugnant, but the refusal to run any risks would amount to giving the Soviet rulers a blank check."[10] And, in his basic treatise on foreign policy, he added:

> Much as we deplore it, most historical changes have been brought about to a greater or lesser degree by the threat or use of force. Our age faces the paradoxical problem that because the violence of war has grown out of all proportion to the objectives to be achieved, no issue has been resolved. We cannot have war. But we have had to learn painfully that peace is something more than the absence of war.[11]

The change in attitude between then and now may seem subtle, but it is fundamental. Kissinger's détente is conceived as a no-risk policy: it aims not merely at avoiding war or the risk of war, but at eliminating all risk of confrontation that could eventually generate a risk of war. Kissinger the public official could find no more severe a critic of his policy of détente than Kissinger the scholar, who would say that the search for a no-risk policy is self-defeating, that a so-called no-risk policy incurs the greatest risk of all.

---

[8] Speech to the Pilgrims of Great Britain, *Department of State Bulletin*, December 31, 1973, p. 779.

[9] *A World Restored*, p. 1.

[10] *Nuclear Weapons and Foreign Policy* (New York: Harper and Brothers, for the Council on Foreign Relations, 1957), p. 4.

[11] *Necessity for Choice*, p. 170.

Risk aversion has gained ascendancy all the same, and along with it reactive diplomacy.[12] Hence Kissinger's previous exhortations to the West to take the initiative in diplomacy, to stand fast on principle, to place the onus of failure on the Soviet Union, to insist on unification of Germany and full preservation of Allied rights in Berlin, to isolate East Germany, to deny legitimacy to Soviet hegemony in Eastern Europe—all have become inconsistent with détente. The emphasis on institutional as opposed to personal diplomacy has been reversed, and summitry has become the standard operating procedure.

Secretary Kissinger hails agreements that Professor Kissinger would have strenuously opposed. Some are acclaimed as landmarks in détente: ratification of the status quo in Berlin, recognition of East Germany, and legitimization of the existing political order in Eastern Europe. SALT I is called an unqualified success in limiting nuclear arms even though it permits a sizable expansion of the Soviet arsenal and contains serious terminological loopholes, both the product of Soviet intransigence. The Soviet Union, once portrayed as a revolutionary power beyond reassurance and incapable of compromise, is now viewed as a conciliatory member of the family of nations practicing restraint in its economic, political, and military relations with others.

One can only speculate on what caused such a profound change in outlook. A case can be made that Kissinger simply saw no other way to turn as he watched the tide of history sweep away, one by one, the elements he had identified as essential for establishing an international order. No progress had been made in resolving the German question, so that Atlantic unity may have seemed beyond reach. Frustration may have become complete when West Germany launched the Ostpolitik, as he had feared it would, and thereby effectively abandoned the cause of reunification, coming to terms instead with the existing order of things in Eastern Europe. A collapse of will and a scramble for accommodation on the part of other Western nations may well have seemed in the offing. Finally, for one reason or another, the strategy of limited warfare proved a dismal failure, tearing American society apart in the process. Little remained out of which to build the edifice of peace envisaged by Kissinger the scholar.

---

[12] The opening to China is a notable exception. Mediation in the Middle East may also seem to be, but our diplomatic efforts there, while obviously intensive and innovative, have clearly been reactive since they were brought into motion only by eruption of the October War and imposition of the Arab oil embargo.

It should be noted that, despite all the other changes in his thinking, Kissinger has not wavered in his insistence on strong conventional forces to defend Europe. He has steadfastly opposed any reduction in U.S. forces and pressed for a buildup in European military strength. We must, he seems to be saying, keep a military anchor to windward while groping for a steady political course.

But all that is speculation. Kissinger has publicized quite a different rationale for détente, one that makes no reference to the evolution of his own thinking, let alone what may have stimulated it. If détente is an imperative, the official statements say, it is also an opportunity for building an international order conducive to peace, for "the United States and the Soviet Union, after decades of profound suspicion, have perceived a common interest in avoiding nuclear holocaust and in establishing a web of constructive relationships." [13] Diplomacy need only take advantage of the relaxation of tensions to create, within the spreading environment of global interdependence, a web of mutual involvement and vested interest. The forecast progression is to be from détente to mutual involvement, then to world community, and finally to world society. The evolving order will acquire legitimacy because the great powers will recognize that they stand to lose more in the way of critical vested interests than they would gain if they defied the rules of international conduct and broke the bonds of interdependence. How fortunate, then, that détente is necessary, for it is also good.

Whereas Kissinger stressed in his scholarly days that diplomacy plays only a symbolic role in a revolutionary age, he now argues that negotiation with the Soviet Union will result in great substantive achievements. The diplomacy of détente is based on the principle of linkage, which means something quite different from what one might think. Normally, linkage is used to describe a quid-pro-quo relationship: an action by one country is linked to a reciprocal action by another. But to Kissinger linkage means the interrelationship between issues, which he explains as follows:

> Our approach proceeds from the conviction that, in moving forward across a wide spectrum of negotiations, progress in one area adds momentum to progress in other areas. If we succeed, then no agreement stands alone as an isolated accomplishment vulnerable to the next crisis. We did not invent the interrelationship between issues expressed in the

---

[13] Speech to the American Legion, *Department of State Bulletin*, September 16, 1974, p. 375. See also his speech to the U.N. General Assembly, *Department of State Press Release*, no. 496 (September 22, 1975), p. 4.

so-called linkage concept; it was a validity because of the range of problems and areas in which the interests of the United States and the Soviet Union impinge on each other. We have looked for progress in a series of agreements settling specific political issues, and we have sought to relate these to a new standard of international conduct appropriate to the dangers of the nuclear age. By acquiring a stake in this network of relationships with the West, the Soviet Union may become more conscious of what it would lose by a return to confrontation. Indeed, it is our hope that it will develop a self-interest in fostering the entire process of relaxation of tensions.[14]

In other words, one thing leads to another, and, once the network of relations is established, the Soviet Union risks losing it all if it renounces any part.

This approach is one of moving diplomatically "along a broad front" rather than step by step, settling one issue at a time. There is no reckoning of quid pro quo, either for each agreement or for the outcome as a whole. The only criterion to be met is that each arrangement should derive from mutual interest and dispense mutual benefit. There is no need for concern if the Soviet Union gains more than the West along the way since the fundamental balance of power will not be altered by such incidental marginal adjustments. What is important is that the Soviet Union, the unruly power being tamed, perceive sufficient gain from the ultimate network of relations to be induced, for fear of losing the gain, to behave in accord with agreed rules of international conduct. Part of the unfolding diplomatic process is the joint declaration from time to time of principles to guide relations among nations (witness the Moscow Statement of Principles, the Agreement on the Prevention of Nuclear War, and the Helsinki Declaration), the purpose being to accustom nations to the notion of paying attention to agreed rules and gradually to establish a sense of obligation to conform to them. The diplomacy of détente should not, he therefore says, be judged piece by piece but as an indivisible process, and the judgment to be rendered is whether a stable international order will emerge from the web of mutual involvement being spun.

Though Kissinger has not put it quite so bluntly, agreements aimed at creating Soviet vested interests in peace will naturally focus on economic and technological issues, since these are the areas of

---

[14] Statement to the Senate Foreign Relations Committee, *Department of State Bulletin*, October 14, 1974, p. 508.

greatest Soviet weakness and hence greatest potential gain. "As political relations have improved on a broad front," he says, "economic issues have been dealt with on a comparably broad front." So far we have concluded "primarily regulatory agreements conferring no immediate benefits on the Soviet Union but serving as blueprints for an expanded economic relationship if the political improvement continued." The prospect is that "over time, trade and investment may leaven the autarkic tendencies of the Soviet system, invite gradual association of the Soviet economy with the world economy, and foster a degree of interdependence that adds an element of stability to the political equation." [15]

Kissinger has never altered his position that transformation of Soviet society, insofar as it takes place, will be a slow evolutionary process essentially beyond the influence of outside pressure. Believing détente to be imperative, he therefore considers it counterproductive, as well as futile, to demand (for example) that Soviet emigration be liberalized as a precondition for improved economic relations. He is not so explicit about why a quid-pro-quo approach should not be used when intervention in domestic affairs is not involved, as would be the case if an economic concession by the United States were offered only in exchange for a political concession by the Soviet Union not directly affecting its internal affairs. Presumably he views such an approach as inconsistent with the commanding objective of constructing a network of mutual interests.

While it would be difficult to exaggerate the significance Kissinger claims for the diplomacy of détente, one should not leave the impression that he considers the envisaged network of interdependency adequate, once built, to preserve the peace by itself. On the contrary, he continues to emphasize that deterrence of aggression, so obviously important today, must remain an essential component of Western policy, new order or not, and that the foundation of deterrence must be built out of strong conventional forces. As in the past, he views SALT as the cornerstone of negotiations with the Soviet Union, having the purpose of stabilizing nuclear parity while preventing an arms race. The question—to which we next turn—is whether deterrence, arms control, and ultimately peace can long coexist with détente.

A Critique

Fault can be found with the very conceptual foundation of Kissinger's grand design: his paradigm of a stable world order. Is legitimacy of

---

[15] Ibid., pp. 511-512.

the international order, conceived as consensus on rules of conduct, synonymous with stability and ultimately with peace? Suppose we reduce the notion to absurdity and let the major powers agree that might makes right—that violence is to be the means for settling disputes. Is this a legitimate and stable order? Or let one power force all others to accept its way of resolving conflict. Is acquiescence the same as consensus?

Clearly, something is missing from Kissinger's paradigm, and the missing element is the ethic of a peaceful order, which involves more than the principle of agreement on rules, for the question immediately arises of how agreement is to be reached and at what cost in terms of other values. If the only goal is an agreed set of rules, why resist the revolutionary power? Why not simply accede to its intransigent demand for a new order? The way out would seem to be simple: if you can't beat 'em, join 'em. But of course that is not the way out, because principles and ideology are at stake.

Kissinger certainly knows this, but he does not face the issue. Perhaps he fears being cast as an ideologue if he reveals his vision of the good society, spelling out the ethical substance he attributes to it. But failure to do so empties his system of moral content and hence deprives it of relevance to the great issues of our time.

This is merely to say that the West has been resisting Soviet expansion, not just to preserve the legitimacy of international relations, but to save Western civilization. The Soviet system menaces a cherished way of life, and the problem has been to find a course of resistance that works—that preserves Western civilization—while avoiding catastrophic war. Kissinger's grand design, by ignoring this moral dilemma, cannot provide a relevant solution to the problem.

Part of the trouble comes from Kissinger's obsession with purity of concept. In his view, a statesman is, for example, either creative or ideological, one or the other. He cannot be both. But why not? The one does not contradict the other: being ideological does not prevent one from being creative or vice versa, even as a matter of degree. Rather, extreme cases aside, the one complements the other, and whether a particular creative process is likely to produce good results or bad can hardly be judged without reference to an underlying ideology. What is the sense of value-free creativity?

This tendency to put concepts into pigeonholes and to pose choices in terms of mutually exclusive alternatives pervades Kissinger's thought. There is either political unity or disintegration, either negotiation or confrontation, either détente or disaster. Nations are either status-quo powers or revolutionary ones; an institution belongs either to an international system or to a domestic structure; a statesman either uses history or is used by it.

Perhaps limited exposure to the subject of economics helps explain this cast of mind. The economist thinks in terms of scarce means, competing uses (values), substitutability and complementarity of goods, comparative advantage, optimal mixes of goods—all quantitative concepts involving more or less of things, not all or nothing. He also reasons stochastically and defines concepts through frequency distributions. Above all, he attributes the unfolding state of affairs more to the operation of impersonal forces than to the activities of specific individuals.

The contrasting modes of analysis may be illustrated by applying them to the issue of what role bureaucracy should play in formulating our foreign policy. Kissinger has been heard to remark that he has yet to find a problem in foreign policy that he could not master if only given time. The trouble is, problems pile up too fast. That is indeed the trouble, but it is faced in many walks of life and resolved through division of labor based on comparative advantage. To solve a problem perfectly but too late—after it has changed with passage of time—is not to solve it at all. Far better to settle for an imperfect but timely solution.

The steward of U.S. foreign relations, no matter how gifted he may be, will have to rely on a large staff if he wants to avoid chaos, and bureaucracy by any other name will perform as poorly. The only question is what kind of bureaucracy it is to be, whether a purely personal staff responsible to the secretary of state, or a composite of personnel drawn from other executive departments. Ours being a government of separated and balancing powers, the purely personal staff is simply not compatible with American political institutions. The point is to prevent excessive concentration of power and the abuse that normally goes with it. Institutional constituencies need to be represented in the formulating of foreign policy precisely because the creative behavior of individual statesmen should conform to institutional constraints and to the consensual process inherent in our system of government. The problem is to avoid free-wheeling statesmanship at the one extreme and hidebound bureaucratic paralysis at the other. Once again, it is a question of proper mix, not of one extreme or the other.

Institutions do not attract Kissinger's attention, for history looms personified before him. There is no evidence of strong interest on his part in comprehending American institutions, their evolution, the forces they exert, or the governmental processes consistent with them.

His writings are essentially bare of reference to such issues: he does not ponder the institutional foundations of various political systems or speculate on the significance of particular institutions. When he contrasts personal and institutional diplomacy, he does not have in mind the nature of the process but the relations being developed, whether they are between individuals or structures. To institutionalized diplomacy he gives the name bureaucratic statesmanship, which he then deplores. Diplomacy simply assumes a personalized shape in Kissinger's eyes.

And so we have the familiar style: personalistic, secretive, mysterious. The public is asked to trust the creative statesman implicitly while he sculpts a new order visible to his mind's eye alone. How can he impart to the masses a comprehension of why and how it will work when it has never existed before?

Perhaps he cannot, but then too bad for creative statesmanship, so called: it is something our political system cannot afford, for nothing is more at odds with the tenets of democracy than the principle of truth by authority. It is not in the American style to bet everything on a horse before knowing its track record and what course it is going to run. American foreign policy must rest on consensus, and it can do so only if its grand design is fully revealed and openly discussed. Similarly, American diplomacy must rest on an institutional foundation, even at the risk of being contaminated by bureaucracy.

Whatever verdict is rendered on the issue of personalized diplomacy, there remains the question, at least equally important, of whether the substance of détente constitutes the best foreign policy for the United States. For brevity, we shall use "détente" to mean the already described configuration of policies and procedures specifically associated with Kissinger's stewardship of foreign affairs, not the relaxation of international tensions in the abstract. The issue is whether détente, so defined, is the best way to preserve the security of the West.

Détente involves a mixed strategy: interdependency is the carrot, deterrence the stick, and arms control the rein. Let us examine the relative importance of these elements, their mutual consistency, and the compatibility of this strategy with the attainment of peace and tranquillity.

Deterrence is obviously the key element, for without it security of the West would depend solely on Soviet good will and self-restraint, scarcely a strong reed to lean upon in the light of Soviet history and ideology. By definition, effective arms control would reduce the level of Western military strength required for deterrence, but the relation between deterrence and interdependency is far more complex. Greater gains from so-called interdependency might, by enhancing the Soviet stake in the existing international order, provide an incentive to the Soviet Union to restrain its expansionist instinct. But the unilateral concessions yielding those gains will cause us to appear all the more weak-willed in the eyes of Soviet leaders, while the gains themselves increase Soviet power commensurately. Soviet leaders will consequently be tempted to seek even greater gains through power politics and to treat the United States as a weakling deserving contempt. Meanwhile, the atmosphere of détente is certain, as we now witness, to sway Western psychology toward downgrading the Soviet threat, cutting defense budgets, and disrupting alliances, the effect being a further tipping of the power balance in the Soviet Union's favor. The dynamics of this process can, as Kissinger once constantly warned, lead to demoralization of the West and Soviet victory by default.

Kissinger's grand design rests on the thesis that the dominating effect of greater interdependency will be to restrain Soviet behavior, but he has little backing from history. Economic interdependence is scarcely new: on the eve of World War I, Norman Angell argued in *The Great Illusion* that the intricate network of world commerce had destroyed all possibility of gain from war. Yet the warring nations of Europe in the twentieth century, as in the nineteenth, normally were close trading partners. As Professor Gregory Grossman reminds us, "history provides little reassurance that trade ensures peace, and Russia's own history least of all. Germany was her largest trading partner just before each of the two World Wars, while China was her largest trading partner (and Russia China's) before the break between Moscow and Peking around 1960." [16]

It is doubtful in any case that the interdependency seemingly envisaged by Kissinger can grow out of normal trading relations, since there is no reason to believe that the Soviet Union is about to abandon its traditional policy of autarky. Soviet planners are, however, eager for a generous infusion of Western technology if the price is right—which is to say, if available on cheap long-term credit or otherwise concessionary terms. The response called for is economic aid, which

---

[16] Gregory Grossman, Statement before the Joint Economic Committee, in *Hearings on the Soviet Economic Outlook*, 93rd Congress, 1st session, July 17-19, 1973, p. 143. In each case, Germany accounted for 40 percent of Russia's foreign trade. On the general issue of trade and peace, see also Albert Wohlstetter, "Threats and Promises of Peace: Europe and America in the New Era," *Orbis*, Winter 1974, p. 1112 ff.

might seem to weld a stronger bond of dependency than a network of trade. But, historically, tribute has been no more successful than trade in preventing conquest or domination by a foreign power.

Perhaps the weakest link in Kissinger's argument is the insistence that any gains accruing to Soviet power from détente are irrelevant "because when both sides possess such enormous power, small additional increments cannot be translated into tangible advantage or even usable political strength." [17] This does not make sense, as Professor Albert Wohlstetter succinctly demonstrates:

> The reasoning supporting this view of the present equilibrium proceeds from the notion that adding an increment of military power to the "overwhelming arsenals of the nuclear age" does not effectively change anything. But is it true that because both the Soviet Union and the United States have many thousands of nuclear warheads, it makes no difference at all if one of the superpowers adds to its arsenal wire-guided anti-tank weapons or surface-to-air missiles or laser-guided bombs or the like for use in limited contingencies? And, can neither gain some political end by transferring such weapons (or even some day a few nuclear weapons) to an ally? On the evidence of October 1973 the Soviet Union feels that one-sided gains are feasible. Statements about the sufficiency or stability of military balances cannot be derived from the mere size of the superpowers' nuclear stockpiles. "Power" is much more complex and varied than that. Neither military nor political nor economic power can be measured by one simple scalar number.[18]

In other words, the power balance is still subject to infinite variation through "marginal adjustments."

Consider what has been happening to Soviet and American defense efforts in real terms. Ours has fallen by almost a sixth since 1964 while theirs (according to our official estimate) has risen by more than a third, coming to surpass ours by 1970. When the incremental cost of the Vietnam War is eliminated, our defense effort shows virtually a steady decline, year by year, since 1963. Theirs shows a steady rise.[19] Are we to believe that this "marginal adjustment" has had no effect on the global power balance?

---

[17] *U.S. Foreign Policy for the 1970's: Shaping a Durable Peace*, A Report to the Congress by Richard Nixon, President of the United States (Washington, D. C.: Government Printing Office, 1973), p. 232.

[18] Wohlstetter, "Threats and Promises of Peace," pp. 1116-1117.

[19] *Annual Defense Report: FY1976 and FY197T* (Washington, D. C.: Government Printing Office, 1975), charts facing I-6 and D-1.

The most immediate impact has been on relative forces in being. In the strategic nuclear sphere, the Soviet Union has moved from a position of substantial inferiority to rough parity, a development that has made the balance of conventional forces, whose importance Kissinger has always stressed, all the more significant. The Soviet Union now has almost twice as many men under arms as we do; a decade ago it had only a sixth more than we did. Our surface combat fleet has shrunk in numbers to become smaller than the Soviet fleet; a decade ago it was a third larger. And so on and on.[20] These divergent trends in military strength surely have implications for diplomacy as well as deterrence, as Kissinger, an avid practitioner of show of force, well knows. And, however unthinkable nuclear war has become, use of conventional force remains habitual: witness the instances of the last quarter century in Korea, Hungary, the Middle East, Africa, South Asia, Cuba, Southeast Asia, Czechoslovakia, and Cyprus.

Over the longer run, diverging defense efforts are likely to disturb the power balance more fundamentally, because the technology of weaponry, offensive and defensive, is in constant flux along with the military arts. There is no way to regulate this dynamic process through arms control without rigorous on-site inspection, and whichever power gains the upper hand in innovation achieves the potential for commanding the future heights of power. The nature of the military balance a decade hence is therefore being determined in the laboratories and on the proving grounds of today. Who knows what new miracles of horror science has in store for us? Perhaps they will metamorphose the balance of terror in the same way that nuclear explosives once did. Whether radical or not, change is certain in military art and science, and relative strength in research and development now is likely to be translated directly into future relative strength in being.

Much more could be said against détente, but it would repeat what can be found in a voluminous literature already in print.[21]

---

20 For relevant data, see ibid., and statement by the chairman, Joint Chiefs of Staff, before the Senate Armed Services Committee on United States Military Posture for FY1975, in *Hearings on S. 300*, 93rd Congress, 2d session, February 5, 1974, part 1.

21 The following are some of the more effective and authoritative critiques of détente: Robert Conquest et al., "Détente: An Evaluation," *Survey*, Spring-Summer 1974, pp. 1-27; Theodore Draper, "Detente," *Commentary*, June 1974, pp. 25-47; Gregory Grossman, Statement before the Joint Economic Committee; and Albert Wohlstetter, "Threats and Promises of Peace."

Enough has been said here to enable us to turn to the questions put by Secretary Kissinger to his critics:

> What is the alternative they propose? What precise policies do they want us to change? Are they prepared for a prolonged situation of dramatically increased international danger? Do they wish to return to the constant crises and high arms budgets of the cold war? Does détente encourage repression—or is it détente that has generated the ferment and the demands for openness that we are now witnessing? Can we ask our people to support confrontation unless they know that every reasonable alternative has been explored? [22]

The questions are quite loaded, of course, because they imply that the critics must choose either white hat or black, either détente or cold war. If that is the only choice open, one wonders what has happened to the "new stable structure of peace" under construction these last six years. As Professor Wohlstetter points out, "what is odd about this metaphor is its desire to have it both ways. The Structure of Peace in the nuclear era is solid and unshakable. Yet we must tiptoe carefully to make sure that we do not bring the whole apparently ramshackle affair crashing down about our ears in the final apocalypse of shattered glass and toppling masonry." [23]

The metaphor is wrong on both counts: the structure is in fact shaky, but there is no need to tiptoe around our relations with the Soviet Union. Not yet. An alternative stance is still achievable for American foreign policy that avoids the perils of Kissinger's détente at the one extreme and stark cold war at the other. It involves restoring Western confidence and resolve, reconstituting deterrence, basing negotiation firmly on the principles of reciprocal concession and unimpaired security, and bargaining accordingly.

As already stressed, Kissinger's diplomacy has created too much one-sided détente, an overrelaxation of tension in the United States and throughout the West. Tension is after all the natural defensive reaction to a perceived threat, and it alerts and stimulates the will to resist. Tension had become excessive in the West, Kissinger concluded, because the cold war associated with it contained a more perilous risk—nuclear annihilation—than the threat being resisted. Tension was relaxed by a diplomatic blitz that had the effect of accenting the nuclear risk while belittling the Soviet threat. The consequence has been a dangerous weakening of the will to resist,

---

[22] Speech in Minneapolis, *Department of State Bulletin*, August 4, 1975, p. 166.
[23] Wohlstetter, "Threats and Promises of Peace," p. 1116.

as a confused public tries to understand whether resistance is unnecessary or whether it is futile.

What needs to be done first is to restore a healthy state of alert based on appreciation of the external dangers threatening the Western way of life and a sense of confidence that they can be overcome. This can be done gradually by nudging diplomacy away from a quest for ways of getting the Soviet Union involved and toward the practice of quid-pro-quo bargaining. The differing nature of Eastern and Western problems provides a basis for reciprocal concessions benefitting both sides while improving Western security, or at least leaving it unimpaired.

The Soviet Union suffers chronically from a defective economy, which constantly thwarts the ambition of Soviet leaders to maximize power in the future as well as now. The economy simply cannot meet the heavy demands placed on it for both maintaining strength in being and providing growth, including a rising living standard. The problems stem from the inefficient organization and deficient incentives of a huge command economy hampered by, among other things, a policy of basic autarky. Hence the economy experiences periodic agricultural crises in the short run and inability to generate a broad front of technological innovation over the long run.

One way out would be fundamental reform of the economic system, but the totalitarian rulers have carefully avoided such a venture for fear of undermining their monolithic power. Curing the patient might eliminate need for the doctor. And so they have turned predictably to the West for help.

Whatever economic help we give is bound to enhance Soviet power—to make it stronger than it otherwise would be. Gains to the West, if any, will be trivial economically and even more so strategically, because Western military and political strength is not constrained significantly by economic factors. Hence we should not help the Soviet Union economically and technologically unless we receive political concessions in return that leave our security at least unimpaired. In general we should insist on improvement of security since what the Soviet Union gains from economic aid and expanded trade strengthens the leadership internally as well as externally. It should be required to reduce the Soviet threat to the West in exchange for the gain in domestic power. It is on this basis that we should parley for Soviet movement on SALT, MBFR, arms control in the Middle East, neutralization of Southeast Asia, and so on.

We must not delude ourselves that our foreign policy has no effect on conditions inside the Soviet Union and Eastern Europe. On this score, Solzhenitsyn is right [24] and Kissinger wrong. If Soviet rulers know the West will bail them out of every economic difficulty, they will be under no pressure to liberalize the regime. Similarly, the relaxing of external tension has always been accompanied in the East by a tightening internally. Kissinger asks whether détente encourages repression or ferment, and the answer is repression. Dissent reached its high mark in the Soviet Union before détente, and the movement has been virtually stamped out since. The various parts of Eastern Europe have experienced a like reactionary policy. Kissinger attacks a straw man when he stubbornly insists that Western foreign policy cannot transform the Soviet domestic structure, for no one seriously believes that outside pressure can cause democracy or anything like it to spring forth overnight in Soviet society. That is not the issue at all, but rather how best to endorse and strengthen the liberal cause in the East.

Businesslike bargaining based on the principle of unimpaired security is hardly confrontation or cold war. If Soviet leaders blindly reject opportunities to make arrangements yielding mutual gains but not undermining our strategic position, we have all the less reason to believe that they will behave responsibly merely to continue enjoying the goodies of involvement.

A revitalized diplomacy will help raise Western morale and confidence and lay the way for repairing our crumbling ramparts and alliances. The downward trend of defense must be reversed or all else is in vain. NATO must be put back together again and its strategic dilemmas resolved. It is a sad fact that Western military strategy has lagged far behind technology, particularly in not appreciating the revolutionary significance of smart weapons, non-nuclear as well as nuclear.[25] Selective strategic targeting, the product of intensive deliberation in the Pentagon in recent years, is an early sign of overdue revision of strategic doctrine.

The issue, then, is how to make best use of our assets in the continuing struggle to defend Western civilization against the threat from the East. Stripped of rhetoric, Kissinger's détente amounts to giving the assets away without requiring any strategic benefits in return, this being done on the premise that the Soviet rulers will so treasure what they are receiving that they will carefully avoid

---

[24] See his Washington speech as reported in *U.S. News and World Report*, July 14, 1975, especially p. 49 ff.

[25] See Wohlstetter, "Threats and Promises of Peace," p. 1122 ff., and Earl Voss, "Defending Europe with Blunderbusses," Reprint 24 (Washington, D. C.: American Enterprise Institute, April 1974).

upsetting the strategic equilibrium. But, as we have argued, they will hardly need to do anything since the power balance will steadily move in their favor anyhow. The alternative proposed here would exchange our assets only for compensatory strategic benefits. Such a diplomacy of reciprocal concession holds far more promise for meaningful peace than the drift of détente.

Epilogue

Yes, there is a grand design to Kissinger's détente, but the West is drifting all the same. Confusion reigns in Congress and the public, and it cannot be dispelled by consensus because diplomacy has become personalized. There is no way for the legitimate organs of government to guide the direction of American foreign policy as long as it conforms to Kissinger's grand design. The policy and his stewardship must both be accepted as a matter of faith.

What Kissinger promises in exchange is peace without risk: he will create a stability of forces and a legitimate international order while eliminating the risk of confrontation between the nuclear superpowers. He promises to do so by entangling the Soviet Union in a web of involvement that it will never wish to escape. The promise cannot be fulfilled.

Kissinger calls his diplomacy creative, but it is more aptly described as romantic. Such statesmanship is rare in the American tradition, which favors a foreign policy resting on idealism and realism, mixed in proportions appropriate to the times.

Above all, American foreign policy is obliged to be public policy, subject to public scrutiny, appraisal, and approbation. Mystery, secrecy, and faits accomplis are simply out of place. If this serious defect is to be remedied, the grand design must go back to the drawing board.

APPENDIX

Excerpts from the Works of
Henry A. Kissinger

1. International Order and Revolution

It is not surprising that an age faced with the threat of thermonuclear extinction should look nostalgically to periods when diplomacy carried with it less drastic penalties, when wars were limited and catastrophe almost inconceivable. Nor is it strange in such circumstances that the attainment of peace should become the overriding concern or that the need for peace should be thought to provide the impetus for its attainment.

But the attainment of peace is not as easy as the desire for it. Not for nothing is history associated with the figure of Nemesis, which defeats man by fulfilling his wishes in a different form or by answering his prayers too completely. Those ages which in retrospect seem most peaceful were least in search of peace. Those whose quest for it seems unending appear least able to achieve tranquillity. Whenever peace—conceived as the avoidance of war—has been the primary objective of a power or a group of powers, the international system has been at the mercy of the most ruthless member of the international community. Whenever the international order has acknowledged that certain principles could not be compromised even for the sake of peace, stability based on an equilibrium of forces was at least conceivable.

Stability, then, has commonly resulted not from a quest for peace but from a generally accepted legitimacy. "Legitimacy" as here used should not be confused with justice. It means no more than an international agreement about the nature of workable arrangements and

For full citations of the sources of the excerpts contained in this appendix, see List of References.

about the permissible aims and methods of foreign policy. It implies the acceptance of the framework of the international order by all major powers, at least to the extent that no state is so dissatisfied that, like Germany after the Treaty of Versailles, it expresses its dissatisfaction in a revolutionary foreign policy. A legitimate order does not make conflicts impossible, but it limits their scope. Wars may occur, but they will be fought *in the name of* the existing structure and the peace which follows will be justified as a better expression of the "legitimate," general consensus. Diplomacy in the classic sense, the adjustment of differences through negotiation, is possible only in "legitimate" international orders.

Whenever there exists a power which considers the international order or the manner of legitimizing it oppressive, relations between it and other powers will be revolutionary. In such cases, it is not the adjustment of differences within a given system which will be at issue, but the system itself. Adjustments are possible, but they will be conceived as tactical manoeuvres to consolidate positions for the inevitable showdown, or as tools to undermine the morale of the antagonist. To be sure, the motivation of the revolutionary power may well be defensive; it may well be sincere in its protestations of feeling threatened. But the distinguishing feature of a revolutionary power is not that it feels threatened—such feeling is inherent in the nature of international relations based on sovereign states—*but that nothing can reassure it.* Only absolute security—the neutralization of the opponent—is considered a sufficient guarantee, and thus the desire of one power for absolute security means absolute insecurity for all the others.

Diplomacy, the art of restraining the exercise of power, cannot function in such an environment. It is a mistake to assume that diplomacy can always settle international disputes if there is "good faith" and "willingness to come to an agreement." For in a revolutionary international order, each power will seem to its opponent to lack precisely these qualities. Diplomats can still meet but they cannot persuade, for they have ceased to speak the same language. In the absence of an agreement on what constitutes a reasonable demand, diplomatic conferences are occupied with sterile repetitions of basic positions and accusations of bad faith, or allegations of "unreasonableness" and "subversion." They become elaborate stage plays which attempt to attach as yet uncommitted powers to one of the opposing systems.

For powers long accustomed to tranquillity and without experience with disaster, this is a hard lesson to come by. Lulled by a period of stability which had seemed permanent, they find it nearly impossible to take at face value the assertion of the revolutionary power that it means to smash the existing framework. The defenders of the status quo therefore tend to begin by treating the revolutionary power as if its protestations were merely tactical; as if it really accepted the existing legitimacy but overstated its case for bargaining purposes; as if it were motivated by specific grievances to be assuaged by limited concessions. Those who warn against the danger in time are considered alarmists; those who counsel adaptation to circumstance are considered balanced and sane, for they have all the good "reasons" on their side: the arguments accepted as valid in the existing framework. "Appeasement," where it is not a device to gain time, is the result of an inability to come to grips with a policy of unlimited objectives.

But it is the essence of a revolutionary power that it possesses the courage of its convictions, that it is willing, indeed eager, to push its principles to their ultimate conclusion. Whatever else a revolutionary power may achieve therefore, it tends to erode, if not the legitimacy of the international order, at least the restraint with which such an order operates. The characteristic of a stable order is its spontaneity; the essence of a revolutionary situation is its self-consciousness. Principles of obligation in a period of legitimacy are taken so much for granted that they are never talked about, and such periods therefore appear to posterity as shallow and self-righteous. Principles in a revolutionary situation are so central that they are constantly talked about. The very sterility of the effort soon drains them of all meaning, and it is not unusual to find both sides invoking their version of the "true" nature of legitimacy in identical terms. And because in revolutionary situations the contending systems are less concerned with the adjustment of differences than with the subversion of loyalties, diplomacy is replaced either by war or by an armaments race.

A World Restored, pp. 1-3.

. . . . A nation will evaluate a policy in terms of its domestic legitimization, because it has no other standard of judgment. But the effort to identify the legitimizing principle of the international order with a parochial version of justice must lead to a revolutionary situation, particularly if the domestic legitimizing principles are sufficiently incommensurable. If a society legitimizes itself by a principle which claims both universality and exclusiveness, if its concept of "justice," in short, does not include the existence of different principles of legitimacy, relations between it and other societies will come to be based on force. For this reason competing systems of legitimacy find it extremely difficult to come to an understanding, not only because they will not be able to agree on the nature of "just" demands, but, perhaps more importantly, because they will not be able to legitimize the attainable international consensus domestically.

A World Restored, p. 328.

. . . . We have never faced up to the fundamental difference between the needs of the West—for example the need for economic assistance in Europe or for enlightened social policies in the United States—and the problems of the emerging nations. In the West, the political and social framework was basically stable. The chief danger was the economic dislocation caused by war or depression. Economic and social programs by removing discontent also permitted the political and social order to be stabilized. But in the new nations the gap between expectations and reality is coupled with the absence of a political structure. Economic programs by themselves are empty if they do not involve also an act of political construction. Indeed, economic assistance, to the extent that it is effective, must subvert the existing largely feudal or tribal order. Many of the new nations lack the institutions or the traditions identified with democracy in the West. Their forms of government all too frequently place a premium on demogoguery and encourage the emergence of some form of Caesarism. Our responsibility is not simply to raise the standard of living of the new nations but to make our belief in freedom and human dignity relevant to their special conditions.

The Necessity for Choice, p. 5.

These obstacles to serious negotiations are magnified by Western, and in particular American, attitudes towards negotiating with the Communists. A *status quo* power always has difficulty in coming to grips with a revolutionary period. Since everything it considers "normal" is tied up with the existing order, it usually recognizes too late that another state means to overthrow the international system. This is a problem especially if a revolutionary state presents each demand as a specific, limited objective which in itself may seem quite reasonable. If it alternates pressure with campaigns for peaceful coexistence, it may give rise to the belief that only one more concession stands in the way of the era of good feeling which is so passionately desired. All the instincts of a *status quo* power tempt it to gear its policy to the expectation of a fundamental change of heart of its opponent—in the direction of what seems obviously "natural" to it.

Were it not for this difficulty of understanding, no revolution would ever have succeeded. A revolutionary movement always starts from a position of inferior strength. It owes its survival to the reluctance of its declared victims to accept its professions at face value. It owes its success to the psychological advantage which single-minded purpose confers over opponents who refuse to believe that some states or groups may prefer victory to peace. The ambiguity of the Soviet challenge results in part from the skill of the Soviet leadership. But it is magnified by the tendency of the free world to choose the interpretation of Soviet motivations which best fits its own preconceptions. Neither Lenin's writings, nor Stalin's utterances, nor Mao's published works, nor Khrushchev's declarations has availed against the conviction of the West that a basic change in Communist society and aims was imminent and that a problem deferred was a problem solved.

It is only to posterity that revolutionary movements appear unambiguous. However weak it may be at the beginning, a revolutionary state is often able to substitute psychological strength for physical power. It can use the very enormity of its goals to defeat an opponent who cannot come to grips with a policy of unlimited objectives.

The Necessity for Choice, pp. 173-174.

There is . . . serious doubt about the historical validity of these evolutionary theories. The record regarding the relationship between economic development and a moderate foreign policy, between industrialization and enlightened domestic institutions, between education and the questioning spirit is not nearly so hopeful as is so often suggested. Industrialization did not make Germany less militant; quite the contrary. A rate of economic development exceeding that of any contemporary new nation did not make Japan a peaceful country. The opposition to modern totalitarianism has rarely centered in the bureaucracies or in the universities. The educational system of Germany was one of the glories of the nation. Yet the evidence would indicate that its support of one of the most vicious dictatorships of modern times far outweighed its resistance to it. Nor is the situation very different in the Soviet Union. For many centuries and in many societies education has had the function of indoctrination. It has been conceived as a tool to strengthen state control. On the historical record this attempt has succeeded more frequently than it has failed, particularly if one judges events by the time scale relevant to the life of an individual and not by centuries.

Indeed, there is no country in which democratic institutions developed *after* industrialization and *as a result of* economic development. Where the rudiments of democratic institutions did not exist at the beginning of the industrial revolution, they did not receive impetus from industrial growth. Democracy may be firmly established in contemporary Germany and Japan, but it came about as the result not of evolution but of a catastrophic war. In all the traditional democratic societies, the essentials of the governmental system antedated the industrial revolution. The American Constitution was developed in a largely agricultural society and so were the fundamental institutions of the British system. These institutions were broadened and elaborated as the countries prospered—but their significant features preceded economic development and are not attributable to it.

On the contrary, in so far as there is a relationship between industrialization and the emergence of democracy, it is that in the nineteenth century political freedom was considered a means *to bring about* economic advance. Democracy was then considered the most "progressive" form of government, not only from the moral point of view but also because it was believed to be the most effective system for promoting material welfare. Feudal rule had excluded the most talented and enterprising members of the community from any share in governmental affairs. The mercantile system had hedged economic activity with governmental restrictions, all the more unbearable because those most affected had no voice either in promulgating or in administering them. In these circumstances, democratic theory expressed the desire of the most active members of society to participate in formulating the rules affecting their welfare. . . .

This suggests that industrialization, rather than producing democracy, may remove the economic incentive for it. When the government does not impede economic development but systematically encourages it, the more enterprising members of society, far from opposing the existing system, will identify themselves with it.

The Necessity for Choice, pp. 290-292.

The Metternich system had been inspired by the eighteenth-century notion of the universe as a great clockwork: Its parts were intricately intermeshed, and a disturbance of one upset the equilibrium of the others. Bismarck represented a new age. Equilibrium was seen not as harmony and mechanical balance, but as a statistical balance of forces in flux. Its appropriate philosophy was Darwin's concept of the survival of the fittest. Bismarck marked the change from the rationalist to the empiricist conception of politics.

"The White Revolutionary: Reflections on
Bismarck," p. 909.

For disagreements among sovereign states can be settled only by negotiation or by power, by compromise or by imposition. Which of these methods prevails depends on the values, the strengths, and the domestic systems of the countries involved. A nation's values define what is just; its strength determines what is possible; its domestic structure decides what policies can in fact be implemented and sustained.

Thus foreign policy involves two partially conflicting endeavors: defining the interests, purposes, and values of a society and relating them to the interests, purposes, and values of others.

The policymaker therefore must strike a balance between what is desirable and what is possible. Progress will always be measured in partial steps and in the relative satisfaction of alternative goals. Tension is unavoidable between values, which are invariably cast in maximum terms, and efforts to promote them, which of necessity involve compromise. Foreign policy is explained domestically in terms of justice. But what is defined as justice at home becomes the subject of negotiation abroad. It is thus no accident that many nations, including our own, view the international arena as a forum in which virtue is thwarted by the clever practice of foreigners.

Pacem in Terris Speech, p. 526.

But if this world is better than our fears, it is still far short of our hopes. We have eased many crises; we have not yet eliminated their roots. Our achievements, solid as they are, have not yet resolved the dangers and divisions of the postwar era. We have begun but not completed the journey from confrontation to cooperation, from coexistence to community. We are determined to complete that journey.

American Legion Speech, pp. 375-376.

2. The Present International Context

There can be little doubt that we are living through a revolutionary period. On the physical plane, the power of weapons is out of balance with the objectives for which they might be employed;

as a result, at a moment of unparalleled strength we find ourselves paralyzed by the implications of our own weapons technology. On the political plane, many of the newly independent Powers continue to inject into their international policies the revolutionary fervor that gained them independence. On the ideological plane, the contemporary ferment is fed by the newly awakened hopes and expectations of hitherto inarticulate peoples and by the rapidity with which ideas can be communicated. And the Soviet bloc, eager to exploit all dissatisfactions for its own ends, has given the present situation its revolutionary urgency.

This is true despite the conciliatory statements of the Twentieth Party Congress. For "peaceful coexistence" was not advanced as an acceptance of the *status quo*. On the contrary, it was justified as the most efficient offensive tactic, as a more effective means to subvert the existing order.   "Reflections on American Diplomacy," p. 44.

This is particularly urgent in a revolutionary period like the present, when change is more desired than harmony. Contemporary international relations would, therefore, be difficult at best but they take on a special urgency because never have so many different revolutions occurred simultaneously. On the political plane, the postwar period has seen the emergence into nationhood of a large number of peoples hitherto under colonial rule. To integrate so many new states into the international community would not be a simple matter at any time; it has become increasingly formidable because many of the newly independent states continue to inject into their policies the revolutionary fervor that gained them independence. On the ideological plane, the contemporary ferment is fed by the rapidity with which ideas can be communicated and by the inherent impossibility of fulfilling the expectations aroused by revolutionary slogans. On the economic and social plane, millions are rebelling against standards of living as well as against social and racial barriers which had remained unchanged for centuries. Moreover, all these revolutions have been taking place at a moment when international relationships have become truly global for the first time; there are no longer any isolated areas. Any diplomatic or military move immediately involves world-wide consequences. And these problems, serious enough in themselves, are manipulated by the Sino-Soviet bloc, which is determined to prevent the establishment of an equilibrium and which is organized to exploit all hopes and dissatisfactions for its own ends.

Statesmanship has never faced a more fearful challenge. Diplomacy is asked to overcome schisms unparalleled in scope and to do so at a moment when the willingness to utilize the traditional pressures available to it—even during periods of harmony—is constantly diminishing. To be sure, the contemporary revolution cannot be managed by force alone; it requires a consistent and bold program to identify ourselves with the aspirations of humanity. But when there is no penalty for irresponsibility, the pent-up frustrations of centuries may seek an outlet in the international field instead of in internal development. To the extent that recourse to force has become impossible, the restraints of the international order may disappear as well.

Moreover, whatever the possibilities of identifying ourselves with the aspirations of the rest of humanity, we are confronted by two revolutionary powers, the U.S.S.R. and Communist China, which pride themselves on their superior understanding of "objective" forces and to which policies unrelated to a plausible possibility of employing force seem either hypocrisy or stupidity. Because harmony between different social systems is explicitly rejected by Soviet doctrine, the renunciation of force will create a vacuum into which the Soviet leadership can move with impunity. Because the Soviet rulers pride themselves on their ability to "see through" our protestations of peaceful intentions, our only possibility for affecting their actions resides in the possession of superior force. For the Soviet leadership has made every effort to retain its militancy. It has been careful to insist that no technological discovery, however powerful, can abolish the laws of history and that real peace is attainable only *after* the triumph of communism. "We will bury you," Nikita S. Khrushchev has said, and the democracies would have been spared much misery had they not so often insisted that dictators do not mean what they say. "Political power," Mao Tse-tung has said, "grows out of the barrel of a gun . . . Yes . . . we are advocates of the omnipotence of the revolutionary war, which . . . is good and is Marxist." [1]

The dilemma of the nuclear period can, therefore, be defined as follows: the enormity of modern weapons makes the thought of war repugnant, but the refusal to run any risks would amount to giving the Soviet rulers a blank check. At a time when we have never been stronger, we have had to learn that power which is not clearly related to the objectives for which it is to be employed may merely paralyze the will. No more urgent task confronts American policy than to bring our power into balance with the issues for which we are most likely to have to contend. All the difficult choices which confront us— the nature of our weapons systems, the risks diplomacy can run—

---

[1] Mao Tse-tung, *Selected Works* (New York: International Publishers, 1954), v. 2, p. 272.

presuppose an ability on our part to assess the meaning of the new technology.

Nuclear Weapons and Foreign Policy, pp. 2-4.

. . . . nuclear technology makes it possible, for the first time in history, to shift the balance of power solely through developments *within* the territory of another sovereign state. No conceivable acquisition of territory—not even the occupation of Western Europe—could have affected the strategic balance as profoundly as did the Soviet success in ending our atomic monopoly. Had a power in the past sought to achieve a comparable strategic transformation through territorial expansion, war would have been the inevitable consequence. But because the growth of nuclear technology took place within sovereign territory, it produced an armaments race instead of war.

Nuclear Weapons and Foreign Policy, pp. 5-6.

. . . . Contemporary domestic structures thus present an unprecedented challenge to the emergence of a stable international order. The bureaucratic-pragmatic societies concentrate on the manipulation of an empirical reality which they treat as given; the ideological societies are split between an essentially bureaucratic approach (though in a different realm of reality than the bureaucratic-pragmatic structures) and a group using ideology mainly for revolutionary ends. The new nations, in so far as they are active in international affairs, have a high incentive to seek in foreign policy perpetuation of charismatic leadership.

These differences are a major obstacle to a consensus on what constitutes a "reasonable" proposal. A common diagnosis of the existing situation is hard to achieve, and it is even more difficult to concert measures for a solution. The situation is complicated by the one feature all types of leadership have in common: the premium put on short-term goals and the domestic need to succeed at all times. In the bureaucratic societies policy emerges from a compromise which often produces the least common denominator, and it is implemented by individuals whose reputation is made by administering the status quo. The leadership of the institutionalized ideological state may be even more the prisoner of essentially corporate bodies. Neither leadership can afford radical changes of course for they result in profound repercussions in its administrative structure. And the charismatic leaders of the new nations are like tightrope artists—one false step and they will plunge from their perch.

American Foreign Policy, pp. 42-43.

Is there then no hope for cooperation and stability? Is our international system doomed to incomprehension and its members to mounting frustration?

It must be admitted that if the domestic structures were considered in isolation, the prognosis would not be too hopeful. But domestic structures do not exist in a vacuum. They must respond to the requirements of the environment. And here all states find themselves face to face with the necessity of avoiding a nuclear holocaust. While this condition does not restrain all nations equally, it nevertheless defines a common task which technology will impose on even more countries as a direct responsibility.

Then, too, a certain similarity in the forms of administration may bring about common criteria of rationality . . . Science and technology will spread. Improved communications may lead to the emergence of a common culture. The fissures between domestic structures and the diffcrent stages of evolution are important, but they may be outweighed by the increasing interdependence of humanity.

American Foreign Policy, pp. 45-46.

. . . . The challenge of our time is whether we can deal consciously and creatively with what in previous centuries was adjusted through a series of more or less violent and frequently catastrophic upheavals. We must construct an international order *before* a crisis imposes it as a necessity. *American Foreign Policy,* p. 49.

The traditional criteria for the balance of power were territorial. A state could gain overwhelming superiority only by conquest; hence, as long as territorial expansion was foreclosed, or severely limited, the equilibrium was likely to be preserved. In the contemporary period, this is no longer true. Some conquests add little to effective military strength; major increases in power are possible entirely through developments within the territory of a sovereign state. China gained more in real military power through the acquisition of nuclear weapons than if it had conquered all of Southeast Asia. If the Soviet Union had occupied Western Europe but had remained without nuclear weapons, it would be less powerful than it is now with its existing nuclear arsenal within its present borders. In other words, the really fundamental changes in the balance of power have all occurred *within* the territorial limits of sovereign states. Clearly, there is an urgent need to analyze just what is understood by power—as well as by balance of power—in the nuclear age.

American Foreign Policy, pp. 60-61.

. . . . The world has become militarily bipolar. Only two powers—the United States and the Union of Soviet Socialist Republics—possess the full panoply of military might. Over the next decade, no other country or group of countries will be capable of challenging their physical preeminence. Indeed, the gap in military strength between the two giant nuclear countries and the rest of the world is likely to increase rather than diminish over that period.

Military bipolarity is a source of rigidity in foreign policy. The guardians of the equilibrium of the nineteenth century were prepared to respond to change with counteradjustment; the policy-makers of the superpowers in the second half of the twentieth century have much less confidence in the ability of the equilibrium to right itself after disturbance. Whatever "balance" there is between the superpowers is regarded as both precarious and inflexible. A bipolar world loses the perspective for nuance; a gain for one side appears as an absolute loss for the other. Every issue seems to involve a question of survival. The smaller countries are torn between a desire for protection and a wish to escape big-power dominance. Each of the superpowers is beset by the desire to maintain its preeminence among its allies, to increase its influence among the uncommitted, and to enhance its security vis-à-vis its opponent. The fact that some of these objectives may well prove incompatible adds to the strain on the international system.

But the age of the superpowers is now drawing to an end. Military bipolarity has not only failed to prevent, it has actually encouraged political multipolarity. Weaker allies have good reason to believe that their defense is in the overwhelming interest of their senior partner. Hence, they see no need to purchase its support by acquiescence in its policies. The new nations feel protected by the rivalry of the superpowers, and their nationalism leads to ever bolder assertions of self-will. Traditional uses of power have become less feasible, and new forms of pressure have emerged as a result of transnational loyalties and weak domestic structures.

This political multipolarity does not necessarily guarantee stability. Rigidity is diminished, but so is manageability. Nationalism may succeed in curbing the preeminence of the superpowers; it remains to be seen whether it can supply an integrating concept more successfully in this century than in the last. Few countries have the interest and only the superpowers have the resources to become informed about global issues. As a result, diplomacy is often geared to domestic politics and more concerned with striking a pose than contributing to international order. Equilibrium is difficult to achieve among states widely divergent in values, goals, expectations, and previous experience.

The greatest need of the contemporary international system is an agreed concept of order. In its absence, the awesome available power is unrestrained by any consensus as to legitimacy; ideology and nationalism, in their different ways, deepen international schisms. Many of the elements of stability which characterized the international system in the nineteenth century cannot be re-created in the modern age. The stable technology, the multiplicity of major powers, the limited domestic claims, and the frontiers which permitted adjustments are gone forever. A new concept of international order is essential; without it stability will prove elusive.

American Foreign Policy, pp. 55-57.

The problem of political legitimacy is the key to political stability in regions containing two-thirds of the world's population. A stable domestic system in the new countries will not automatically produce international order, but international order is impossible without it. An American agenda must include some conception of what we understand by political legitimacy. In an age of instantaneous communication, we cannot pretend that what happens to over two-thirds of humanity is of no concern or interest to the United States. This does not mean that our goal should be to transfer American institutions to the new nations—even less that we should impose them. Nor should we define the problem as how to prevent the spread of Communism. Our goal should be to build a moral consensus which can make a pluralistic world creative rather than destructive.

American Foreign Policy, p. 84.

Above all, whatever the measure of power, its political utility has changed. Throughout history increases in military power, however slight, could be turned into specific political advantage. With the overwhelming arsenals of the nuclear age, however, the pursuit of marginal advantage is both pointless and potentially suicidal. Once sufficiency is reached, additional increments of power do not translate into usable political strength, and attempts to achieve tactical gains can lead to cataclysm.

This environment both puts a premium on stability and makes it difficult to maintain. Today's striving for equilibrium should not be compared to the balance of power of previous periods. The very notion of "operating" a classical balance of power disintegrates when the change required to upset the balance is so large that it cannot be achieved by limited means.

More specifically, there is no parallel with the 19th century. Then the principal countries shared essentially similar concepts of legitimacy and accepted the basic structure of the existing international order. Small adjustments in strength were significant. The "balance" operated in a relatively confined geographic area. None of these factors obtain today. . . .

When we refer to five or six or seven major centers of power the point being made is not that others are excluded but that a few short years ago everyone agreed that there were only two. The diminishing tensions and the emergence of new centers of power have meant greater freedom of action and greater importance for all other nations.

In this setting, our immediate aim has been to build a stable network of relationships that offers hope of sparing mankind the scourges of war. An interdependent world community cannot tolerate either big-power confrontations or recurrent regional crises.

But peace must be more than the absence of conflict. We perceive stability as the bridge to the realization of human aspirations, not an end in itself. We have learned much about containing crises, but we have not removed their roots. We have begun to accommodate our differences, but we have not affirmed our commonality. We may have improved the mastery of equilibrium, but we have not yet attained justice. . . .

The opportunities of mankind now transcend nationalism and can only be dealt with by nations acting in concert:

—For the first time in generations mankind is in a position to shape a new and peaceful international order. But do we have the imagination and determination to carry forward this still-fragile task of creation?

—For the first time in history we may have the technical knowledge to satisfy man's basic needs. The imperatives of the modern world respect no national borders and must inevitably open all societies to the world around them. But do we have the political will to join together to accomplish this great end?

Pacem in Terris Speech, p. 530.

Economic interdependence is a fact. We must resolve the paradox of growing mutual dependence and burgeoning national and regional identities.

Pilgrims of Great Britain Speech, p. 779.

3. Diplomacy in a Revolutionary World

But we do live in a period of ideological conflict, and this gives its particular urgency to current international relationships. It is argued on many sides that this ideological conflict can be eliminated by an act of will, that as during the 18th and 19th Centuries, we should conduct international relations without any regard for domestic institutions. But this would be putting the cart before the horse. The Eighteenth Century could consider domestic institutions irrelevant because the governments felt sufficiently secure to ignore domestic transformations abroad and because there did not exist a power which claimed both universality and exclusiveness for its vision of a just social order. From the moment that France insisted on the universal applicability of its maxims and set about to subvert existing institutions, the intricate maneuvers of Eighteenth Century diplomacy failed in limiting the scope of international conflicts. And the diplomatic methods appropriate to the 19th Century proved unequal to the situation after 1918 precisely because World War I had so shaken the structure of the international order that what was at issue was no longer the adjustment of differences within a system of equilibrium, but the equilibrium itself.

"Limitations of Diplomacy," p. 7.

The major weakness of United States diplomacy has been the insufficient attention given to the symbolic aspect of foreign policy. Our positions have usually been worked out with great attention to their legal content, with special emphasis on the step-by-step approach of traditional diplomacy. But while we have been addressing the Soviet leaders, they have been speaking to the people of the world. With a few exceptions we have not succeeded in dramatizing our position, in reducing a complex negotiation to its symbolic terms. In major areas of the world the Soviets have captured the "peace offensive" by dint of the endless repetition of slogans that seemed preposterous when first advanced but which have come to be common currency through usage. The power which has added 120 million people to its orbit by force has become the champion of anticolonialism. The state which has utilized tens of millions of slave laborers as an integral part of its economic system appears as the champion of human dignity in many parts of the world. Neither regarding German unity, nor Korea, nor the satellite orbit have we succeeded in mobilizing world opinion. But Formosa has become a symbol of American intransigence, and our overseas air bases a token of American aggressiveness. We have replied to each new Soviet thrust with righteous protestations of our purity of motive. But the world is not moved by legalistic phrases, at least in a revolutionary period. This is not to say that negotiations should be conceived as mere propaganda; only that, by failing to cope adequately with their psychological aspect, we have given the Soviet leaders too many opportunities to use them against us.

As a result the international debate is carried on almost entirely in the categories and at the pace established by the Soviets. The world's attention is directed toward the horror of nuclear weapons but not toward the danger of Soviet aggression which would unleash them. The Soviet leaders negotiate when a relaxation of tension serves their purpose and they break off negotiations when it is to their advantage, without being forced to shoulder the onus for the failure.

Nuclear Weapons and Foreign Policy, pp. 61-62.

It is not an accident that the diplomatic stalemate has become more intractable as weapons have grown more destructive. Rather than facilitating settlement, the increasing horror of war has made the process of negotiation more difficult. Historically, negotiators have rarely relied exclusively on the persuasiveness of the argument. A country's bargaining position has traditionally depended not only on the logic of its proposals but also on the penalties it could exact for the other side's failure to agree. An abortive conference rarely returned matters to the starting point. Rather, diplomacy having failed, other pressures were brought into play. Even at the Congress of Vienna, long considered the model diplomatic conference, the settlement which maintained the peace of Europe for a century was not achieved without the threat of war.

As the risks of war have become more cataclysmic, the result has not been a universal reconciliation but a perpetuation of all disputes. Much as we may deplore it, most major historical changes have been brought about to a greater or lesser degree by the threat or the use of force. Our age faces the paradoxical problem that because the violence of war has grown out of all proportion to the objectives to be achieved, no issue has been resolved. We cannot have war. But we have had to learn painfully that peace is something more than the absence of war. Solving the problem of peaceful change is essential; but we must be careful not to deny its complexity.

The intractability of diplomacy has been magnified by the polarization of power in the post-war period. As long as the international system was composed of many states of approximately equal strength, subtlety of maneuver could to some extent substitute for physical strength. As long as no nation was strong enough to eliminate all the others, shifting coalitions could be used for exerting pressure or marshaling support. They served in a sense as substitutes for physical conflict. In the classical periods of cabinet diplomacy in the eighteenth and nineteenth centuries, a country's diplomatic flexibility and bargaining position depended on its availability as a partner to as many other countries as possible. As a result, no relationship was considered permanent and no conflict was pushed to its ultimate conclusion. Disputes were limited by the tacit agreement that the maintenance of the existing system was more important than any particular disagreement. Wars occurred, but they did not involve risking the national survival and were settled in relation to specific, limited issues.

The Necessity for Choice, pp. 170-171.

4. Limited War

The dilemma of the nuclear period can, therefore, be defined as follows: the enormity of modern weapons makes the thought of war repugnant, but the refusal to run any risks would amount to giving the Soviet rulers a blank check. At a time when we have never been stronger, we have had to learn that power which is not clearly related to the objectives for which it is to be employed may merely paralyze the will. No more urgent task confronts American policy than to bring our power into balance with the issues for which we are most likely to have to contend. All the difficult choices which confront us— the nature of our weapons systems, the risks diplomacy can run— presuppose an ability on our part to assess the meaning of the new technology.

Nuclear Weapons and Foreign Policy, p. 4.

The power of modern weapons thus forces our statesmanship to cope with the fact that absolute security is no longer possible. Whatever the validity of identifying deterrence with maximum retaliatory power, we will have to sacrifice a measure of destructiveness to gain the possibility of fighting wars that will not amount to national catastrophe. Policy, it has been said, is the science of the relative. The same is true of strategy, and to understand this fact, so foreign to our national experience, is the task history has set our generation.

Nuclear Weapons and Foreign Policy, p. 117.

. . . . The end result of relying on purely military considerations is certain to be all-out war: the attempt to render the enemy defenseless.

A limited war, by contrast, is fought for specific political objectives which, by their very existence, tend to establish a relationship between the force employed and the goal to be attained. It reflects an attempt to *affect* the opponent's will, not to crush it, to make the conditions to be imposed seem more attractive than continued resistance, to strive for specific goals and not for complete annihilation.

. . . Since the military can never be certain how many forces the opponent will in fact commit to the struggle and since they feel obliged to guard against every contingency, they will devise plans for limited war which insensibly approach the level of all-out conflict.

From a purely military point of view they are right, for limited war is essentially a political act. Its distinguishing feature is that it has no "purely" military solution. The political leadership must, for this reason, assume the responsibility for defining the framework within which the military are to develop their plans and capabilities. To demand of the military that they set their own limits is to set in motion a vicious circle. The more the military plan on the basis of crushing the enemy even in a limited area, the more the political leadership will recoil before the risks of taking *any* military action. The more limited war is conceived as a "small" all-out war, the more it will produce inhibitions similar to those generated by the concept of massive retaliation. The prerequisite for a policy of limited war is to reintroduce the political element into our concept of warfare and to discard the notion that policy ends when war begins or that war can have goals distinct from those of national policy. . . .

The purpose of limited war is to inflict losses or to pose risks for the enemy out of proportion to the objectives under dispute. The more moderate the objective, the less violent the war is likely to be. This does not mean that military operations cannot go beyond the territory or the objective in dispute; indeed, one way of increasing the enemy's willingness to settle is to deprive him of something he can regain only by making peace. But the result of a limited war cannot depend on military considerations alone; it reflects an ability to harmonize political and military objectives. An attempt to reduce the enemy to impotence would surely lead to all-out war. . . .

There exist three reasons, then, for developing a strategy of limited war. First, limited war represents the only means for preventing the Soviet bloc, at an acceptable cost, from overrunning the peripheral areas of Eurasia. Second, a wide range of military capabilities may spell the difference between defeat and victory even in an all-out war. Finally intermediate applications of our power offer the best chance to bring about strategic changes favorable to our side. . . .

. . . The Sino-Soviet bloc can be turned back short of general war in one of two ways: by a voluntary withdrawal or by an internal split. The former is unlikely and depends on many factors beyond our control, but the latter deserves careful study.

While it is impossible to predict the precise circumstances of a possible split within the Soviet orbit, its general framework can be discerned. The U.S.S.R. may be forced to loosen its hold on its European satellites if it finds that the effort to hold them in line absorbs ever more of its strength. And relations between China and the Soviet Union may become cooler if the alliance forces either partner to shoulder risks for objectives which are of no benefit to it.

Nuclear Weapons and Foreign Policy, pp. 120-126.

Limited war is not simply a question of appropriate military forces and doctrines. It also places heavy demands on the discipline and subtlety of the political leadership and on the confidence of the society in it. For limited war is psychologically a much more complex problem than all-out war. In an all-out war the alternatives will be either surrender or unqualified resistance against a threat to the national existence. To be sure, psychological factors will largely determine the relative willingness to engage in an all-out war, and the side more willing to run risks may gain an important advantage in the conduct of diplomacy. However, once the decision to fight is taken, a nation's physical ability to conduct war will be the most important factor in the outcome.

In a limited war, on the other hand, the psychological equation will be of crucial importance, not only with respect to the decision to enter the war but throughout the course of military operations. A limited war among major powers can be kept limited only by the conscious choice of the protagonists. Either side has the physical power to expand it, and to the extent that each side is willing to increase its commitment in preference either to a stalemate or to a defeat, the war will gradually become an all-out one. The restraint which keeps a war limited is a psychological one: the consequences of a limited victory or a limited defeat or a stalemate—the three possible outcomes of a limited war—must seem preferable to the consequences of an all-out war. . . .

. . . A policy of limited war therefore presupposes three conditions: the ability to generate pressures other than the threat of all-out war; the ability to create a climate in which survival is not thought to be at stake in each issue; and the ability to keep control of public opinion in case disagreement arises over whether national survival is at stake. The first condition depends to a considerable extent on the flexibility of our military policy; the second on the subtlety of our diplomacy; the third will reflect the courage of our leadership. . . .

. . . It is important for our leadership to understand that total victory is no longer possible and for the public to become aware of the dangers of pressing for such a course.

A long history of invulnerability has accustomed us to look at war more in terms of the damage we can inflict than of the losses we might suffer. The American people must be made aware that with the end of our atomic monopoly all-out war has ceased to be an instrument of policy, except as a last resort, and that for most of the issues likely to be in dispute our only choice is between a strategy of limited war or inaction. It would be tragic if our government were deprived of freedom of maneuver by the ignorance of the public regarding the consequences of a course from which it would recoil if aware of all its implications. This is all the more true since the same ignorance which underlies the demand for all-or-nothing solutions might well produce panic if our people were unexpectedly brought face-to-face with the consequences of an all-out war. Conversely, a public fully aware of the dangers confronting it and forearmed psychologically by an adequate civil defense program will be better prepared to support a more flexible national policy.

Nuclear Weapons and Foreign Policy, pp. 139-143.

. . . . deterrence cannot be separated from strategy. Deterrence depends not only on the extent of the retaliation to aggression but also on its likelihood. These two factors are related to each other in an inverse ratio. If either is very low, deterrence fails. If the side seeking to deter emphasizes the destructiveness of its response at the expense of the likelihood of retaliation, aggression may be encouraged. If too much stress is placed on a strategy of minimum cost, the penalties against aggression may be too low for effective deterrence. Deterrence is at a maximum when the product of these two factors is greatest. The challenge before our military policy is to strike the best balance between deterrence and the strategy we are prepared to implement should deterrence fail. . . .

The purpose of a strategy of limited war, then, is first to strengthen deterrence and, second, if deterrence should fail, to provide an opportunity for settlement before the automatism of the retaliatory forces takes over. The *worst* that could happen if we resisted aggression by means of limited war is what is *certain* to happen if we continue to rely on the strategy of the past decade. . . .

However paradoxical it may seem, the danger of escalation is one of the chief reasons why a strategy of limited war contributes to deterrence and also why, if deterrence fails, there is a chance of keeping a conflict limited. A strategy of limited war adds to deterrence for the very reason usually invoked against it. The danger that a limited war may expand after all works both ways. An aggressor may not credit our threat of massive retaliation because it would force us to *initiate* a course of action which will inevitably involve enormous devastation. He may calculate, however, that once engaged in war on any scale neither he nor we would know how to limit it, whatever the intentions of the two sides. The stronger the limited war forces of the free world, the larger will have to be the Communist effort designed to overcome them. The more the scale of conflict required for victory approaches that of all-out war the greater will be the inhibitions against initiating hostilities. In this sense a capability of limited war is necessary in order to enhance the deterrent power of the retaliatory force. . . .

Nevertheless, it would be irresponsible to minimize the risk of escalation. It will be great in proportion as limited war is conceived entirely as a strategic problem rather than an opportunity for a pause to permit negotiations. Limited war should not be considered a cheaper method of imposing unconditional surrender but an opportunity for another attempt to prevent a final showdown. We must enter it prepared to negotiate and to settle for something less than our traditional notion of complete victory. To be sure, the most likely outcome of a conflict fought in this manner is a stalemate. But the high likelihood of a stalemate would seem to deprive aggression of its object. Hence deterrence would be achieved. . . .

. . . as the missile age develops, an inadequate limited-war establishment may combine the worst features of every strategic choice. If we place only a *little step* between surrender and all-out war, the Soviet opportunity to blackmail the free world will substantially remain. The dread alternative of surrender or suicide will even be compounded by the risk of a series of "small" defeats, none of which seems "worth" an all-out war. The consequences may be positive Communist incentive to defeat small American limited-war forces—if only to demonstrate our impotence. In the approaching period of mutual invulnerability, the United States cannot impose on itself the burden of having to respond to every challenge with the threat of self-destruction. And it only fudges the issue to look at the limited-war establishment primarily as a trigger for the retaliatory force. The free world will not be really safe until it can shift on to the aggressor the risk of initiating all-out war. . . .

However, our alternatives are quite different. No responsible person advocates *initiating* limited war. The problem of limited war will arise only in case of Communist aggression or blackmail. In these circumstances, if we reject the concept of limited war, our only options will be surrender or all-out war. And it does not make sense to ridicule the notion of limited war because it *might* lead to general war and then to rely on a military policy which gives us no other choice but all-out war. The conclusion is almost inescapable that in case of Soviet aggression—the only contingency worth discussing in this context—many of those ridiculing the concept of limited war would prefer surrender to resistance. . . .

There are three prerequisites for a strategy of limited war: (1) the limited war forces must be able to prevent the potential aggressor from creating a *fait accompli*; (2) they must be of a nature to convince the aggressor that their use, while involving an increased risk of all-out war, is not an inevitable prelude to it; (3) they must be coupled with a diplomacy which succeeds in conveying that all-out war is not the sole response to aggression and that there exists a willingness to negotiate a settlement short of unconditional surrender.

The Necessity for Choice, pp. 58-65.

A *fait accompli* changes the attempt to *prevent* a given event, which is the basis of deterrence, to an effort to *compel* a certain course of action. Once a *fait accompli* exists, the purpose of strategy is no longer to induce a potential aggressor to refrain from attacking. It must force him to withdraw. In deciding to attack, the psychological burden is on the aggressor: he must take an affirmative step and his hesitation will be great in proportion as the objective seems unattainable. Once the aggressor is in possession of his prize, however, the psychological burden shifts in his favor. The defender must now assume the risk of the first move. The aggressor can confine himself to outwaiting his opponent. The aggressor becomes more committed to his prize the longer he is in possession of it, while his opponent's incentive to persevere is diminished with every day that the *fait accompli* endures. When resisting occupation, the defender has the option of persevering in self-defense or surrendering. When the aggressor has already gained his objective, the defender can have peace by settling for the new *status quo*. In all limited-war strategies save that of local defense, the psychological balance is in favor of the aggressor and will become so increasingly the longer the conflict lasts. This is because only local defense can prevent a *fait accompli*. . . .

Building up a capability for local defense is a complex but not insoluble task, made all the more necessary by the starkness of the alternatives. The rewards are high. To a considerable extent, a strategy of local defense will lift from the West the impossible choices of current military policy. It will increase the flexibility of Western diplomacy. It is the prerequisite of effective arms control negotiations. For as long as there is a wide disparity in local power, the Soviet Union will not have an incentive for serious arms control. In devising a strategy of local defense, however, we come up squarely against one of the great unresolved issues of Western military policy: the relative significance of nuclear and conventional weapons.

The Necessity for Choice, pp. 72-75.

Some years ago this author advocated a nuclear strategy [*Nuclear Weapons and Foreign Policy*, p. 174 ff]. It seemed then that the most effective deterrent to any substantial Communist aggression was the knowledge that the United States would employ nuclear weapons from the very outset. A nuclear strategy appeared to offer the best prospect of offsetting Sino-Soviet manpower and of using our superior industrial capacity to best advantage.

The need for forces capable of fighting limited nuclear war remains. However, several developments have caused a shift in the view about the relative emphasis to be given conventional forces as against nuclear forces. These are: (1) the disagreement within our military establishment and within the alliance about the nature of limited nuclear war; (2) the growth of the Soviet nuclear stockpile and the increased significance of long-range missiles; (3) the impact of arms control negotiations. The first of these considerations raises doubts as to whether we would know how to limit nuclear war. The second alters the strategic significance of nuclear war. The third influences the framework in which any strategy will have to be conducted and determines the political cost. . . .

The factors will create an extremely precarious situation if the free world continues to rely primarily on a nuclear strategy. The more the pressures against *any* use of nuclear weapons build up, the greater will be the gap between our deterrent policy, our military capability, and our psychological readiness—a gap which must tempt aggression. The years ahead must therefore see a substantial strengthening of the conventional forces of the free world. If strong enough to halt Soviet conventional attacks—as in areas such as Europe they could be—conventional forces would shift the onus and risk of initiating nuclear war to the other side. Even where they cannot resist every scale of attack, they should force the aggressor into military operations on a major scale. They would thereby make ultimate recourse to nuclear weapons politically and psychologically simpler, while affording an opportunity for a settlement before this step is taken. . . .

Conventional forces should not be considered a substitute for a limited nuclear war capability but as a complement to it. For against an opponent equipped with nuclear weapons, it would be suicidal to rely entirely on conventional arms. Such a course would provide the precise incentive an aggressor needs to employ nuclear weapons and to sweep all before him. A conventional war can be kept within limits only if nuclear war seems more unattractive. . . .

Whatever the significance of prolonged mobilization in the era of what is now called conventional technology, it becomes an extremely risky course in the nuclear age. When both sides possess nuclear weapons, there is always the danger that they will be used regardless of declarations and perhaps even intentions. The risk of escalation is a product of two factors: the nature of the limitations and the duration of the conflict. A limited nuclear war lasting one day may involve a smaller danger of escalation than a conventional war lasting a year. Aggression may be tempted by the prospect of dramatic initial victories and the possibility that the free world may not be willing to run the risks of nuclear war inherent in a prolonged mobilization.

Forces-in-being are therefore more important than at any previous time in our history. This does not mean that they must be able to hold every square inch of every threatened area. It does indicate that enough of an area must be protected so that the governments concerned consider resistance not simply a quixotic gesture. And the prospect of restoring the situation must be sufficiently imminent so that the aggressor sees no prospect in creating a *fait accompli* and then "out-enduring" his opponents. In short, greater reliance on a conventional strategy implies that we are prepared to maintain conventional forces and mobilizable reserves in a higher state of readiness than ever before. It is as dangerous to think of a conventional strategy in which nuclear weapons could somehow be eliminated from our calculations as it is to continue to consider nuclear weapons from the perspective of our now-ended invulnerability. . . .

The nuclear age has not repealed the principle that actions speak louder than words. We should make immediate and energetic efforts to restore the conventional forces of the free world. We must adjust our doctrine accordingly. But it would be extremely risky to create the impression that we would acquiesce in a conventional defeat in vital areas. Once the conventional balance of forces were restored, we could then responsibly announce that we would employ nuclear weapons only as a last resort and even then in a manner to minimize damage. To the extent that the Communists are unable to defeat the conventional forces of the free world without resorting to nuclear weapons, the practical effect will be our renunciation of the first use of nuclear weapons. Even where this is not the case, strengthened conventional forces would pose an increased risk for the aggressor and provide opportunities either for the mobilization of additional conventional forces or for negotiations before we take the decision to use nuclear weapons. The inability to defend every area with conventional forces should not be used as an excuse for failing to build up our strength. The free world must not become a victim of asserting that if it cannot do *everything* it will not do *anything*. . . .

. . . the price of flexibility is sacrifice and effort. If our military establishment continues to be built around nuclear weapons and if we refuse to make the sacrifices involved in greater reliance on conventional weapons, the current emphasis of arms control negotiations must be shifted. In such circumstances it will not be wise to lump all nuclear weapons into a separate category of special horror. Rather we should then elaborate as many distinctions between various types of uses and explosive power as possible in order to mitigate the consequences of nuclear war. On the other hand, if we really believe in the need for a greater emphasis on conventional weapons, we must be prepared to accept the paradox that the best road to nuclear arms control may be conventional rearmament.

This is not to say that arms control should be reserved for the nuclear field. On the contrary, the balance in conventional forces should be based on a combination of increase of our conventional strength and control schemes to stabilize an agreed level of forces. But we cannot rely on arms control as a *substitute* for an effort in the conventional field. For, if the disparity in local power becomes too great, the Soviet Union will lose any incentive for responsible negotiations. No scheme of arms control will then seem to enhance its security as much as its existing superiority. And the requirements of inspection become excessive when the strategic position of one or both sides is so precarious that it can be overthrown by even a minor violation.

The Necessity for Choice, pp. 81-94.

5. Alliances and the Atlantic Community

The security problem of Europe may be summed up as follows: (a) The Soviet Union can threaten all of Europe from its own territories. Consequently, alliances are not essential for its safety. (b) No European country alone is capable of withstanding Soviet pressure. Security is therefore inseparable from unity. (c) The threat of all-out war is losing its credibility and its strategic meaning. (d) The defense of Europe, therefore, cannot be conducted solely from North America, because the aggressor can pose threats which will not seem to warrant total retaliation and because, however firm allied unity may be, a nation cannot be counted on to commit suicide in defense of a foreign territory.

The Necessity for Choice, pp. 105-106.

Two general solutions present themselves: one based on the North Atlantic Community as a whole, the other on a more closely integrated Europe. If the North Atlantic Community can increase its political cohesion so that it begins to approach a federal system, the control of nuclear weapons and their location will become much less urgent problems. The deployment of NATO forces will then become an essentially *technical* issue. The only meaningful debate will concern the best dispositions of *common* weapons for the *common* welfare. Once it becomes clear that even a minor threat against Europe will engage the United States as fully as a minor threat against Alaska, temptations for Soviet pressure will be substantially reduced. Once our allies are convinced that a threat against what they consider their vital interests will be treated in fact like an attack on the United States, one of the prime motives for developing independent retaliatory forces will disappear. Great Britain and the United States do not have a moral right to deplore the acquisition of nuclear weapons by their allies unless they are prepared to take drastic steps in the direction of greater political integration. The minimum condition is to move in the direction of a North Atlantic confederation. . . .

If a NATO nuclear establishment proves unfeasible and if national possession by our European allies is politically dangerous and militarily useless, what alternative presents itself? In default of the NATO solution described above, the most hopeful approach would seem to be a European Atomic Force into which the British and soon-to-be French retaliatory forces would be merged. If they pool their resources, the European powers including Great Britain will possess sufficient resources to create a substantial nuclear establishment. To be sure, Europe could not win an all-out war with the U.S.S.R. even by striking first. But it might deter, through the ability to extract an exorbitant price in case of aggression. The price would be exorbitant when even a successful nuclear war with Europe might weaken the Soviet Union to the point where it would become inferior to the United States and thus vulnerable to a preemptive attack. As a result, there would be no incentive to use nuclear weapons against Europe alone. And an attack against Europe and the United States simultaneously should lead to unacceptable damage from a retaliatory blow. A European Atomic Force—provided it was well protected— might not only deter a nuclear attack, it could also furnish an umbrella for a conventional defense. . . .

A modification of the system of control over nuclear forces will remain empty, however, unless NATO is prepared to make greater efforts to strengthen its local defenses, particularly in the conventional field. As long as NATO relies on a modified version of massive retaliation, no arrangement for control of nuclear weapons can overcome the inherent weakness and lack of credibility of such a course.

The Necessity for Choice, pp. 121, 125, 127.

Whatever aspect of the Atlantic alliance is considered, the goal of Western policy must be to develop greater cohesion and a new sense of purpose. We are living in a period which, in retrospect, will undoubtedly appear to be one of the great revolutions in history. The self-sufficient nation-state is breaking down. No nation—not even the largest—can survive in isolation or realize its potentialities, material, political, or spiritual, on its own.

Nowhere is this more evident than in the Atlantic community. None of the major problems with which the nations surrounding the North Atlantic are confronted can be finally resolved on a national basis. On the contrary, policies of petty nationalist advantage will prove equally disastrous to everyone. The security problem is insoluble on a national basis. The attempt to achieve security by unilateral efforts will produce impotence.

The Necessity for Choice, pp. 165-166.

The cohesion of the West, in short, can no longer be assured simply by improving the co-ordination of national policies. It requires also structural changes within the Western alliance. It seems time to examine carefully the possibility of creating federal institutions comprising the entire North Atlantic community, however attenuated these may be at first.

The Necessity for Choice, pp. 166-167.

In the past, the Soviet threat has often produced Atlantic unity. It may again. But ultimately the unity of the West depends on what we affirm, not on what we reject. We of the West, who bequeathed the concept of nationalism to others, must summon the initiative and imagination to show the way to a new international order. Nothing is more crucial than for the West to develop policies which make of it a true community.

The Necessity for Choice, p. 168.

All the realities of human aspirations and of a technology of global impact require a close association of the nations bordering the North Atlantic. But Western history is full of tragedies, where a basic community of interests has been submerged by subsidiary rivalries or insufficient understanding. Ancient Greece foundered on this dilemma. Western Europe nearly tore itself apart before it discovered its underlying unity. And now the nations bordering the North Atlantic face the perennial problem of the West: Whether they can generate sufficient purpose to achieve community without first experiencing disaster.

The Troubled Partnership, p. 28.

Alliances, to be effective, must meet four conditions: (1) a common objective—usually defense against a common danger; (2) a degree of joint policy at least sufficient to define the *casus belli*; (3) some technical means of cooperation in case common action is decided upon; (4) a penalty for noncooperation—that is, the possibility of being refused assistance must exist—otherwise protection will be taken for granted and the mutuality of obligation will break down.

In the system of alliances developed by the United States after the Second World War, these conditions have never been met outside the North Atlantic Treaty Organization (NATO). In the Southeast Asia Treaty Organization (SEATO) and the Central Treaty Organization (CENTO), to which we belong in all but name, there has been no consensus as to the danger. Pakistan's motive for obtaining U.S. arms was not security against a Communist attack but protection against India. The Arab members of CENTO armed not against the U.S.S.R. but against Israel. Lacking a conception of common interests, the members of these alliances have never been able to develop common policies with respect to issues of war and peace. Had they been able to do so, such policies might well have been stillborn anyway, because the technical means of cooperation have been lacking. Most allies have neither the resources nor the will to render mutual support. A state which finds it difficult to maintain order or coherence of policy at home does not increase its strength by combining with states suffering similar disabilities. . . .

In short, our relations with Europeans are better founded on developing a community of interests than on the elaboration of formal legal obligations. No precise blueprint for such an arrangement is possible because different fields of activity have different needs. In the military sphere, for example, modern technology will impose a greater degree of integration than is necessary in other areas. Whatever their formal autonomy, it is almost inconceivable that our allies would prefer to go to war without the support of the United States, given the relatively small nuclear forces in prospect for them. Close coordination between Europe and the United States in the military sphere is dictated by self-interest, and Europe has more to gain from it than the United States.

For this very reason, it is in our interest that Europeans should assume much greater responsibility for developing doctrine and force levels in NATO, perhaps by vitalizing such institutions as the West European Union (WEU), perhaps by alternative arrangements. The Supreme Allied Commander should in time be a European.

Military arrangements are not enough, however. Under current conditions, no statesman will risk a cataclysm simply to fulfill a legal obligation. He will do so only if a degree of *political* cooperation has been established which links the fate of each partner with the survival of all the others. This requires an entirely new order of political creativity. . . .

Finally, under present circumstances, an especially meaningful community of interests can be developed in the social sphere. All modern states face problems of bureaucratization, pollution, environmental control, urban growth. These problems know no national considerations. If the nations of the Atlantic work together on these issues—through either private or governmental channels or both—a new generation habituated to cooperative efforts could develop similar to that spawned in different circumstances by the Marshall Plan.

American Foreign Policy, pp. 65-66, 75-77.

6. The German Question

Finally, it is important to remember that Germany is the last country which should be encouraged to be "flexible." Germany's attempt to pursue an isolated policy in the center of the Continent has brought disaster to Europe twice in a generation. If it is once more placed in the position to make arrangements with both sides— the political expression of neutrality—it will also be capable of menacing both sides, if only by the threat of a change of front. Such a Germany would hardly be conducive to peace and stability in Europe. Western policy must seek to retain Germany as a willing member of European political and economic institutions, whatever the ultimate security arrangements.

"The Search for Stability," p. 555.

The ideal situation would be a Germany strong enough to defend itself but not strong enough to attack, united so that its frustrations do not erupt into conflict and its divisions do not encourage the rivalry of its neighbors, but not so centralized that its discipline and capacity for rapid action evoke countermeasures in self-defense. Such a Germany has existed only at rare periods. To help establish it must be a major task of Western policy.

But can one talk realistically of the unification of Germany? Is this not one of the issues which seem to be ignored by tacit agreement? It is often maintained that acceptance by the West of the *status quo* in Eastern Europe and especially in Germany is the key to stability in Europe. We are urged to recognize facts we are powerless to change in any case. We are told that once Soviet rule in Eastern Europe is formally accepted, the Soviet Union will be a "satisfied" power no longer interested in expansion.

The notion that wisdom consists of adjustment to facts is, of course, hardly a heroic one. Pressed to its extreme, it implies a policy without goal and measures without conception. It places the direction of events in the hands of those strong enough and ruthless enough to bring about a "fact." Nothing in the world would ever have been changed were adjustment the sole rule of conduct.

The Necessity for Choice, p. 129.

No doubt the division of Germany is likely to persist whatever the Western policy. No brilliant plan is likely to produce unification. The issue, however, is not only whether unification can be achieved but what attitude the West should take toward this "fact." Should it in effect co-operate with Soviet repression of freedom in Eastern Germany by formally accepting the division of Germany? Or should it strive to force the Soviets to accept the onus for thwarting Germany's national aspirations? . . . The question remains whether we should cap the omissions of the past with a formal recognition of the East German regime. It does not make too much sense to use the errors of the past to justify new mistakes.

The Necessity for Choice, p. 130.

. . . . If the Federal Republic is persuaded that it cannot achieve reunification through ties to the West, it may attempt separate dealings with the East. Unification could then be used by the Soviets as a lure to ending, step by step, the achievements of European integration and to encouraging a race for Moscow's favor. Alternatively, there may be a resurgence of virulent nationalism. The argument will gain credence that close ties with the West having failed, Germany must pursue a policy of pressure and nationalistic advantage.

The Necessity for Choice, p. 132.

Obviously, the [Soviet] draft [of a peace] treaty is conceived to be the beginning, not the end of a process. Recognition of the East German regime would bring about a situation where in the future any change in Germany would have to be to the disadvantage of the West. It would foreclose unification on a democratic, but not on a Communist basis. The minimum result would be a severe disillusionment in the Federal Republic. The Communists could then attempt to cajole or threaten West Germany into a "neutralist" course. If this failed, they could withdraw recognition from the Federal Republic as "fascist" or as betraying the interests of the German people and deal with the East German regime as the representative of *all* of Germany. If the West had previously recognized the East German satellite, it could hardly retaliate by withdrawing its recognition without exposing itself to the charge of cynical power politics and of using the principle of self-determination for tactical ends only. Having given up a position which was morally and politically unassailable, we would become hostages of future Soviet moves. We would be forced to contest the issue of Germany on ever more unfavorable ground.

The Necessity for Choice, p. 134.

But what about the Soviet demand that the future of Germany be settled by negotiation between the two Germanys? The cynicism of this proposal is matched only by the readiness of too many in the West to take it seriously. It is hardly to be supposed that the subservient satellite whose government would be eliminated as a result of German unification will prove any more tractable on the issue of resolving the division of Germany than its patron in the Kremlin. Even if the two German governments were to negotiate with each other in "good faith"—whatever is the significance of that phrase in this particular context—the result would undoubtedly be an increase rather than a decrease of tension. . . . Confederation is thus a euphemism for recognizing East Germany. It is not a means of unifying Germany but a device by which the West accepts the division of Germany.

The Necessity for Choice, p. 135.

These considerations bear importantly on the question of Berlin. For the issue in Berlin is not whether a city completely surrounded by Communist territory is "worth" a war—as is often asserted. Berlin has become the touchstone of the West's European policy. A defeat for the West—that is, a deterioration of Berlin's possibility of living in freedom—could not help but demoralize the Federal Republic. It would mark the end to any hope for reunification. The scrupulously followed Western-oriented policy would be seen as a fiasco. This would become a warning to all other states in Europe of the folly of resisting Communist pressure. Berlin would illustrate the irresistible nature of the Communist advance to the rest of the world. Whatever their view of the merits of the issue, the uncommitted would come to believe that the protection of the West is illusory, that wisdom, if not ideological sympathy, counsels adjustment to Communist standards. And even in the relations of some of these states to each other, a Western defeat in Berlin would serve to increase tensions. The precarious peace which is being maintained between the Arab states and Israel in part by the fear of Western intervention against aggressive acts might not long survive a demonstration of Western impotence in Europe.

The Necessity for Choice, p. 139.

Can the status of Berlin be safeguarded in return for the recognition of East Germany? Such a result would be an enormous Communist victory. The Communists would gain international recognition for the partition of Germany and create a situation whereby they alone could emerge as the advocates of unification. The Federal Republic would be dealt a staggering blow for reasons already described. And for all of this the West would obtain a withdrawal of a unilateral, unprovoked threat. This is hardly a procedure calculated to discourage further Communist pressure.

Recognition might not even suffice to obtain a temporary guarantee for West Berlin. For the negotiating process is not symmetrical. Once we offered recognition, we would have given up the principle of self-determination. If the Communists then raised their demands, they would have transformed the question of recognition from a matter of principle into a question of negotiating expedients. Once we agreed that recognition was simply a problem of haggling over conditions, the Communists would have every reason to expect that they could exact it sooner or later, if not from us then from some of our allies.

The Necessity for Choice, p. 144.

. . . acceptance by the West of the division of Germany as permanent would upset the domestic equilibrium of the Federal Republic; this is one of the reasons that the Soviets are so eager to secure Western recognition of the status quo in Germany. The division of Germany may be unavoidable; but the cohesion of the Atlantic Alliance requires that there is no ambiguity about the reason for it. If the West tacitly or explicitly abandoned the principle of German national unity—by collaborating with the Soviets to keep Germany divided—Germans would consider it a sacrifice of their basic interests. No German political leader can accept as permanent the subjugation of 17 million of his compatriots—all German political parties are agreed on this point. His minimum goal must be to ameliorate conditions in East Germany—a goal that he will be under increasing pressure to pursue independently if his allies prove indifferent to it.

The Troubled Partnership, pp. 68-69.

. . . as German activity toward the East increases, the fear of another Rapallo may create a vicious circle. Germany's Western neighbors will draw closer together; they may also seek to anticipate the Federal Republic by speeding up their own contacts with Moscow. This cannot be in the interest of either Atlantic or European cohesion; in the long run it will prove disastrous for the Federal Republic as well, because it may lead to its eventual isolation.

Only a united Atlantic Alliance facing jointly the issue of Germany's future can minimize the danger of a sharp conflict between Germany's national goals and its Atlantic ties. The effort to devise a common German policy is essential not only in order to retain

Germany as a willing member of the Alliance, but also for the peace of Europe as well. It is against all probability that a large and dynamic country can be kept divided indefinitely in the center of the continent that gave the concept of nationalism to the world. As long as two German states exist, they are bound to interact with each other. If they consider that their social and political systems are incompatible, each will be driven to try to subvert the other. Since they contain the same basic population and a similar tradition, each has unusual scope for doing so. The Soviet formula that the two German states should settle their own future is a short-sighted, if clever, move to consolidate the status quo. It guarantees that sooner or later events will move beyond the control of either East or West—and perhaps of the Germans themselves. The permanent division of Germany into hostile, competing states is inherently dangerous. If Germany's neighbors to the East understand their own interests, they will realize that the present course may have the gravest long-term consequences.

The Troubled Partnership, pp. 215-216.

A precondition of any negotiating program is an agreed strategy toward Eastern Germany. Specifically, should the West seek to ameliorate conditions in the so-called German Democratic Republic by increasing contacts with it or by isolating it? The latter course seems the most promising and the one most consistent with a long-term policy on German unification.

The Troubled Partnership, p. 217.

The long-term hope for German unity resides in an evolution in the West that will act as a magnet for the countries of Eastern Europe. As Western Europe achieves political unity, the fear of any one state will diminish. A united Europe, moreover, will be a powerful magnet for the countries of Eastern Europe. As ties between the two parts of Europe grow, the East German satellite could increasingly appear as a vestige of a passing era.

"The Price of German Unity," p. 17.

Berlin's potential as Europe's perennial flashpoint has been substantially reduced through the quadripartite agreement of 1971. The United States considers strict adherence to the agreement a major test of détente.

Statement to Senate Foreign Relations
Committee, p. 516.

7. Arms Control

.... It is ... no longer possible to speak of military superiority in the abstract. What does "being ahead" in the nuclear race mean if each side can already destroy the other's national substance? What is the strategic significance of adding to the destructiveness of the nuclear arsenal when the enormity of present weapons systems already tends to paralyze the will?

Nuclear Weapons and Foreign Policy, pp. 114-115.

Because we lack a strategic doctrine and a coherent military policy, it is inevitable that our proposals on arms control are fitful. We are in no position to know whether a given plan enhances security, detracts from it, or is simply irrelevant. As a consequence, proposals are developed as a compromise between competing groups and without an over-all sense of purpose. Instead of urging disarmament conferences because we wish to advance a scheme in which we have confidence, we have reversed the process: typically we have been forced to assemble a set of hasty proposals because we have agreed to go to a conference under the pressure of world opinion or Soviet diplomacy. The confusion is demonstrated by the fact that, though our military establishment is built around nuclear weapons, our arms control negotiations have stigmatized the strategy on which we have been relying. To conduct both policies simultaneously is clearly disastrous.

The Necessity for Choice, p. 4.

.... Arms control negotiations must not become a device for the unilateral weakening of the West. A scheme for European security, therefore, must take care not to wreck NATO, for without NATO each European country would face the preponderant Soviet might alone. It must not eliminate the possibility of local defense, lest our allies become demoralized by the threat of Soviet conventional and tactical nuclear strength. But while protecting our European allies against nuclear blackmail or conventional aggression, it must also give assurances to the Soviet Union against attack from NATO territory. The question then becomes whether it is possible to conceive of two military establishments on the Continent capable of defensive action but deprived through appropriate control measures of offensive power.

The Necessity for Choice, p. 149.

The political benefits of less ambitious schemes such as "thinning out" of forces are even more problematical. Such a measure, whatever its significance for purposes of arms control, affords no possibility of lessening Soviet political control in the satellites or in East Germany. For purposes of political control two Soviet divisions are as effective as twenty: they symbolize Soviet power and they establish the possibility, if not the right, of intervention.

The Necessity for Choice, pp. 152-153.

On the military side, many of the proposals for arms control in Central Europe are designed to prevent any change in the military *status quo*. For example, a freeze on the level of forces in Central Europe or a "thinning out under appropriate inspection" has been proposed. Apart from the fact that the importance of inspection is vastly overrated in this context—existing intelligence in Central Europe being quite good—most of these schemes fail to come to grips with the real security problem. They do not affect significantly the capability of the United States or the Soviet Union, or even of Western Europe, to launch a sudden all-out attack. At the same time, since present or planned NATO forces are already inadequate for offensive ground operations, most schemes for troop reduction would merely weaken the capability for local defense of the West without providing an additional reassurance to the Soviet Union. They would improve the *offensive*, but not the *defensive*, position of the U.S.S.R. Even a troop freeze could keep NATO from adapting itself to changed strategic relationships. Unless coupled with a major reduction of Soviet forces or a build-up of conventional strength in the part of the Continent outside the controlled zone and probably through a combination of both, it will perpetuate an inequality which will represent a growing invitation to Soviet adventures as Soviet long-range missiles multiply.

The Necessity for Choice, p. 153.

Two conclusions follow:

First, the inadequacies of the current NATO effort may cause the Soviets to believe that they can gain no additional security from arms control schemes or that they can achieve the objectives of arms control through unilateral Western actions. They may not take Western proposals seriously because they believe themselves already protected by their local preponderance. Thus, effective negotiations may be prevented, not by the strength of NATO but by its weakness and irresolution.

Second, schemes for arms control in Europe cannot by themselves eliminate the problems which are caused by the Soviet suppression of freedom in Eastern Europe and particularly in East Germany. As long as Germany remains divided, the danger of an explosion exists, whatever the wishes of the chief protagonists. Measures to control armaments in Central Europe, to be effective, should therefore accompany a political settlement. The natural dividing line for arms control schemes is the Oder, not the Elbe. The two problems of German unity and arms control in Europe are thus closely related. Unification without a scheme for arms control will frighten all the states surrounding Germany. A European security system without German unification is either a palliative or it will magnify conflicts in Central Europe.

The Necessity for Choice, p. 157.

To be sure, short of a major policy reversal, the Soviet Union would derisively reject any such proposals. But the reason is not that they would fail to contribute to stability. Rather it is that the Soviet Union is reluctant to give up its East German puppet, its springboard for wrecking NATO and for the eventual domination of all of Germany. The melancholy fact may be that in their present state of mind the Soviet leaders are interested only in those agreements in Europe which contribute to instability.

The Necessity for Choice, pp. 158-159.

If serious negotiations are possible between the free world and the Communist states, arms control would seem the obvious subject. . . .

. . . . with modern technology, arms—at least certain types of them—are themselves a factor of tension. As a result arms control acquires a new significance. . . .

The importance of arms control measures is therefore beyond dispute. Effective schemes may well arrest a slide towards a cataclysm. They could reduce the risks of accidental war. They may prevent, or at least slow down, the spread of nuclear weapons. If the two sides cannot give expression to this community of interests by proposing concrete, serious programs, little hope exists for negotiations on other subjects. . . .

Also, arms control to be meaningful must be devised in relation to the technological factors which produce the need for it. It cannot be conceived in a fit of moral indignation. Effective schemes require careful, detailed, dispassionate studies and the willingness to engage in patient, highly technical negotiations. Otherwise arms control may increase rather than diminish insecurity. Much as arms control may be desired, it must not be approached with the attitude that without it all is lost. The consequence of such a conviction must be to encourage the Communists to seek to use arms control negotiations primarily for psychological warfare in order to demoralize the West. The belief may grow that if negotiated agreements prove impossible, unilateral disarmament must be attempted. Arms control, in short, should be a device to enhance stability, not a prelude to surrender.

The Necessity for Choice, pp. 210-213.

. . . . The goal of responsible arms control measures must be to determine, free from sentimentality, not how to eliminate retaliatory forces but how to maintain an equilibrium between them. It is more worthwhile—at least for the immediate future—to seek to reduce the incentive to attack rather than the capability for it. . . .

The discussion about nuclear disarmament has revealed the paradoxical fact that there is a certain safety in numbers. And this is true even if both sides scrupulously observe an agreement to limit nuclear weapons or the means of delivery. Instability is greater if each side possesses 10 missiles than if the equilibrium is stabilized at, say, 500. For an attack which is 90 per cent successful when the defender has 10 missiles leaves him one—or a number hardly likely to inflict unacceptable damage. An attack of similar effectiveness when the defender possesses 500 missiles leaves 50—perhaps sufficient to pose an unacceptable risk in retaliation. And of course it is technically more complicated to destroy such a large number. Reduction of numbers is thus not an infallible remedy. A very small and vulnerable retaliatory force may increase the danger of war by encouraging the opponent to risk surprise attack.

It follows that stability is greatest when numbers are sufficiently large to complicate the calculations of the aggressor and to provide a minimum incentive for evasion but not so substantial that they defeat control. The efficacy of a control scheme to limit numbers thus depends on the answers to two queries: What advantage will the side violating the agreement gain through its first violation? How difficult is the system to inspect for violations?

The Necessity for Choice, pp. 215, 217.

In order to develop criteria for an effective inspection system, it is necessary to consider again the objectives of an effective scheme to control surprise attacks:

1. The opposing strategic striking forces should be stabilized at a level which reduces to a minimum the incentive to attack.

2. The inspection system should be reliable enough to prevent evasions which can upset the strategic balance, yet not so pervasive as to destroy the security of the retaliatory force.

The Necessity for Choice, p. 223.

In the first case—conflict among smaller countries—an international police force can be highly useful. There are potential trouble spots, such as the Middle East, where the major nuclear powers would prefer to avoid a conflict but where direct intervention is impossible for political or psychological reasons. Or else actual crises can occur where the intervention of the major powers would exacerbate tensions and increase the dangers of a holocaust. In such situations an international police force can make a major contribution, precisely because the major powers agree—at least to the extent of seeking a mechanism to avoid a showdown.

The Necessity for Choice, p. 234.

A scheme for dealing with local aggression must therefore meet these requirements: (a) It must establish an equilibrium of forces suitable for local war through a combination of build-up in the West, reduction in the Communist countries, and inspected ceilings on manpower. Though this appears to be one-sided, it is the condition of stability. The less desirable alternative is a unilateral Western build-up to be followed by a control scheme. (b) It must be coupled with an inspection system adequate to monitor the level of forces within acceptable limits of error. (c) It must provide for zonal limitations, because local aggression depends not only on the size of the forces but on their deployment.

The Necessity for Choice, p. 239.

. . . . To undertake a major program of controlling nuclear weapons without restoring the balance of conventional forces is sheer irresponsibility.

The Necessity for Choice, p. 254.

Before we can advance serious proposals we have to clarify our purposes. It is said that we must engage in arms control to free resources for the *real* competition, which is in the field of economics. It is claimed that arms control may reduce the burden of taxation. Arms control is advocated as a means of speeding up the evolution of the Soviet system. Involved explanations are advanced that we can trust the Soviet Union to observe any agreement.

Almost all these arguments are essentially irrelevant. The Soviet leaders can hardly be attracted by schemes whose primary purpose is announced to be the transformation of their system. Useful schemes ought not to depend on whether or not we can trust the Soviet leaders—indeed, if we could trust them, they might be less important. Arms control schemes will be effective if they contain their own incentive for observation and if there can be confidence, not in the other side but in the control arrangements.

The argument about freeing resources for economic competition begs the principal question, which is, after all, precisely whether it is possible to develop arms control measures which promote stability and achieve this end. . . .

We must not confuse collateral with primary goals. The purpose of arms control is to enhance the security of *all* parties. Any attempt to achieve a unilateral advantage must doom arms control. Similarly, neither reduction of forces nor inspection can be an end in itself. The test of any agreement is whether it adds to or detracts from stability, whether it makes war less likely or more so. No collateral benefits will be able to compensate for badly conceived control measures. . . .

At the same time, however dedicated we may be to arms control, it is important not to approach it with the attitude that a failure of negotiations will inevitably doom humanity. Such a conviction is bound to produce pressures for unilateral disarmament and therefore remove any incentive for serious negotiations on the part of the Communists. If the Soviet leaders are convinced that the fear of war overrides all other considerations, two consequences will follow. They will be encouraged to engage in the most violent threats in order to demoralize the free world further. And they will become convinced that arms control is unnecessary since they are already protected by the free world's fears. Paradoxical as it may seem, a measure of instability in the arms race is required to provide an impetus for arms control. . . .

If we are to make progress in the field of arms control, the military establishment must come to understand that in the present state of technology an arms race is the most unstable of all forms of security, and that properly conceived arms control must increase the security of *all* countries. And many enthusiasts for arms control must realize that ardor is no substitute for precision. A great deal depends on the ability to be concrete. In the next few years we may have perhaps our last opportunity to stabilize the arms race by means of negotiation. Perhaps Communist obduracy will foil our most earnest efforts. But it would be unforgivable if we failed because we refused to face either the importance or the complexity of the challenge.

The Necessity for Choice, pp. 283-286.

8. Relations with Communist Powers

If these trends continue, the future of freedom will be dim indeed. It is difficult for Americans to visualize national disaster. Yet the outlines of what may be ahead are not too difficult to discern. Tempted by the growing disparity in power the Soviet Union will bring pressure on all surrounding areas. The loss in ideological dynamism will be more than compensated by the increasing opportunities presented by our weakness. Communist policy will alternate between protestations of peaceful intentions and spasms of intransigence designed to demoralize the West. Negotiations will turn into a kind of psychological warfare. If the West can be humiliated over a period of time, the new nations, whatever their moral preference, will consider Communism the wave of the future. The success of Moscow and Peiping will have the same kind of attraction as the accomplishments of Europe in the nineteenth century. No amount of economic assistance will avail against the conviction that the West is doomed. Considerations of national interest, of wishing to be "progressive," will bring about an accommodation to Communist wishes. . . .

As the free world gains in purpose, cohesion and safety, the Communist approach to negotiations may alter. Instead of using arms control negotiations to tempt or blackmail the West into unilateral disarmament, the Communist leaders may address themselves seriously to the problem of how to reduce the tensions inherent in an unchecked arms race. Then coexistence may become something other than a slogan. But whatever Communist purposes may be, our task is essentially the same: to define for ourselves the nature of a peace consistent with our values and adequate for our security.

The Necessity for Choice, pp. 6-7.

Negotiations with Communist leaders are complicated by one of the key aspects of Leninist theory: the belief in the predominance of "objective" factors. One of the proudest claims of the Communist leaders is that in Marxist-Leninist theory they possess a tool enabling them to distinguish appearance from reality. "True" reality consists not of what statesmen say but of the productive processes—the social and economic structure—of their country. Statesmen, particularly capitalist statesmen, are powerless to alter the main outlines of the policy their system imposes on them. Since everything depends on a correct understanding of these "objective factors" and the relation of forces they imply, "good will" and "good faith" are meaningless abstractions. One of the chief functions of traditional diplomacy—to persuade the opposite party of one's view point—becomes extremely difficult when verbal declarations are discounted from the outset.

The Necessity for Choice, pp. 172-173.

Thus, whatever aspect of the Soviet system they have considered, many in the West have sought to solve our policy dilemma by making the most favorable assumptions about Soviet trends. At one time, we drew comfort from the fact that the Soviet leaders required peace in order to devote themselves to building up their economy. A decade and a half later, a more benign Soviet policy was predicted with exactly the opposite argument. Now the already accomplished industrialization was thought to give the Soviet leaders too much of a stake in their society for them to risk foreign adventures.

Our concern with the transformations of Soviet society causes us to be either too rigid or too accommodating. It makes us overlook that we have to deal in the first instance with Soviet foreign and not with its domestic policy. From the notion that a settlement depends on a change in Soviet society, it is not a big step to the view that liberalization of Soviet society is equivalent to a settlement. In such an atmosphere, it is not surprising that a controversy should have raged about the desirability of relaxing tensions but not about the conditions which would make such a relaxation meaningful, about the need for peace but not about the elements of stability, about the level at which we should talk but not what we should discuss once we get there.

The Necessity for Choice, pp. 199-200.

A responsible approach to negotiations must be quite different. We should make no unjustified concessions to a Soviet leader simply because we consider him to be liberal. We should not refuse to make concessions, which are otherwise desirable, simply because we consider a Soviet leader Stalinist. The ultimate test in either case is whether a given measure enhances stability or detracts from it. Above all, our measures should not be so dependent on either the Kremlin's smiles or its frowns. Negotiations with the Soviet Union must be justified by our purposes, not theirs. If the Soviet Union really wants a settlement, negotiations will reveal this. If Soviet overtures to end the Cold War are a tactical maneuver, a purposeful diplomacy should be able to make Soviet bad faith evident.

The Necessity for Choice, pp. 202-203.

. . . . if we can only offer what the Soviet leaders have indicated they will accept, the framework of every conference will be established by the other side and the terms of the settlement will be Soviet terms. Or else agreement will become an end in itself. Negotiations gravitate towards problems which seem "soluble"—often only because of their unimportance.

Pushed too far, such an approach implies the surrender of all judgment. It will cause us to fail in one of the major tasks of a revolutionary period: to make clear to the people of the free world the nature of the issues in dispute. While all possibilities of a settlement must be explored, it is equally necessary to develop conviction about the problems that are impossible to solve. It is important for us to be conciliatory if the Soviet leaders should be prepared to negotiate seriously. But it is no less crucial that we force them to bear the onus for their failure to accept responsible proposals.

The Necessity for Choice, p. 204.

Diplomacy thereby becomes a form of Soviet political warfare. For if we can negotiate only on issues that the Soviet leaders have declared soluble, it is not surprising that the attention of the world is focused on the symptoms rather than the causes of the difficulties: on NATO, but not the Soviet hostility which produced it; on the all-too-inadequate Western defense effort, but not on the preponderant Soviet strength which called it forth; on the dangers to peace in case of another satellite upheaval, but not on the Soviet repression without which the danger of upheaval would not exist; on the Soviet scheme for total disarmament, but not on more meaningful proposals which might have some prospect of slowing down the arms race; on the Congo or Cuba, but not on Hungary, Tibet or East Germany. The illusion is created that the Cold War can be ended by proclamation.

The Necessity for Choice, p. 206.

A lasting settlement is possible only if the Soviet leaders become convinced that they will not be able to use the West's desire for peace to demoralize it. If they are serious about their desire to avoid war, they must realize that negotiations can be used for purely tactical purposes only so often and that, measured against the dangers of such a course, the gains they may score are paltry. We in turn should strive to demonstrate to the Soviet leaders that they have a real policy decision to make which we will do everything possible to ease. They must face the fact that the policy of applying relentless pressures on the West creates untold perils for all the peoples of the world. On the other hand, they must be convinced that they can increase their security through negotiation. Should they seriously seek a settlement, they would find us flexible and conciliatory.

Negotiations are important. But it is essential to conduct them without illusions. We do not need to postulate a basic Soviet transformation in order to believe in the possibility of a settlement. Nor is it a prerequisite to successful negotiation to pretend that a relaxation of tensions is primarily within Western control. The West must have much more positive goals than to divine Soviet intent. We do ourselves an injustice if we make an issue of the desirability of relaxing tensions or of ending the Cold War. The test of conciliatoriness does not reside in interpreting Soviet trends in the most favorable manner. Nor does it consist of proving the desirability of peace—which should be taken for granted. Rather, the challenge which confronts the West is to determine what are the possibilities of a settlement which does not hazard our security and is consistent with our values. Only in the purposeful is flexibility a virtue.

The Necessity for Choice, p. 209.

A fundamental transformation is particularly difficult as long as the Communist ruling groups remain reasonably alert to the task of recruiting the ablest people into their ranks. A revolution always has two prerequisites: a grievance against the existing order and a group of people capable of leadership and willing to pay the price of opposition. The liberal revolutions of the eighteenth and nineteenth centuries were the result of the exclusion of the ablest and most energetic group—the bourgeoisie—from participation in the affairs they considered most significant. Since there was no way by which the most talented people could be integrated or achieve respect, they were a ready-made reservoir of leadership for all opposition. The same group also organized the Russian Revolution.

However, when a career is available to the talented within the existing structure, only the most dedicated will take the road of rebellion and accept the social ostracism which it might involve. The temptation is nearly overwhelming, even for those with serious reservations about the existing system, to seek to improve it from within rather than to overthrow it. The more educated they are and the greater their stake is in society, the more they may prefer a form of collaboration to risking everything on outright opposition. A major obstacle to a dramatic change in the Communist system is posed by the systematic Soviet attempt to integrate the ablest individuals into the existing order through preferment, indoctrination, propaganda, and if necessary, pressure. By constantly recruiting the most talented into its ranks, the Communist hierarchy deprives any opposition of its potential leadership. . . .

This is not to say that an evolution in Communist societies is impossible. On the contrary, it is inevitable. No system of government is immune to change. No country has ever maintained an unaltered social structure. But the nature of the transformation is by no means foreordained. It can move towards liberalization; but it can also produce the gray nightmare of *1984*. It can lead to the enhancement of freedom; it may also refine the tools of slavery. Moreover, the mere fact of a transformation is not the only concern of our generation. Equally important is the time scale by which it occurs. It was, after all, no consolation for Carthage that 150 years after its destruction Rome was transformed into a peaceful *status quo* power.

The Necessity for Choice, pp. 298-300.

It is as idle to expect Communism, which has been expanding for over a quarter of a century, to transform itself into a democratic government, as was Lenin's opposite assumption that Communism was an evolutionary successor to democracy. To establish a democratic government of the Western type in the Soviet Union would require not evolution but a revolutionary upheaval. Though change is inevitable, the possibility of influencing it directly is rapidly diminishing. Whatever influence we have will depend less on what we say or even on specific acts of policy than on the creativity of our performance domestically and internationally. If we can be sufficiently vital, the leaders in Communist societies may in time seek to imitate what comes to be considered a more "progressive" system. But the key point is that after a certain stage of evolution the sources of the impetus for change from *within* the system are sharply restricted.

This is why the theories developed in both Great Britain and the United States that even a world-wide triumph of Communism would not prevent an eventual triumph of the values of liberty are so disingenuous. In the face of nuclear war, it is perhaps possible to understand an attitude which places survival above all else. However, it is unforgivable to seek to buttress this conviction with evolutionary theory. It is one thing to assert that war is suicidal. It is quite another to argue that it is possible to have all the benefits of surrender plus the advantage of an automatic evolutionary development which will safeguard our values. Relying on history to ameliorate a despotism is simply a way of deferring to another generation the sacrifices which are likely to become more difficult and perhaps meaningless as time goes on. What would have been Western history if the knights who defeated the Arabs at Tours had surrendered because they believed in the historic inevitability of the triumph of Christianity? Central Europe would today be Moslem. And while some sort of evolutionary development would undoubtedly have taken place, what we consider Western civilization would not have come into being. One can debate the historic significance of this. But there is no sense pretending that there are no turning points and only different roads towards a similar goal.

The Necessity for Choice, pp. 307-308.

. . . . Anyone succeeding in Communist leadership struggles must be single-minded, unemotional, unsentimental and dedicated. Nothing in the experience of Soviet leaders would lead them to prize peace as an end or to accept protestations of personal goodwill at face value. Their own career—indeed their survival—has been advanced by the ability to dissemble. Khrushchev's success, as Brezhnev's after him, depended on his ability to hide his ambition until it was too late for his rivals to organize against him. Suspiciousness is therefore inherent in the domestic position of Soviet leaders. It is unlikely that their attitude toward the outside world is more benign. There is no reason for them to treat foreign statesmen more gently than their own colleagues or to expect more consideration from them.

The Troubled Partnership, p. 195.

The Sino-Soviet split was the catalyst for the overt fragmentation of the Communist world. The causes of this rift are many and complex. There is the rivalry of two empires along the most extended land frontier of the world. Competition for a dominant role in the underdeveloped countries plays a part. But what makes the dispute insoluble is the conflict over the leadership of the world Communist movement. While the actual manifestations of the rift may be patched up from time to time, its underlying cause seems beyond repair. A movement that claims to represent a universal truth cannot tolerate two centers of orthodoxy. As long as Peiping rejects the doctrinal pre-eminence of Moscow, the most important reason for discord will persist—whatever temporary adjustments may be made.

The Troubled Partnership, pp. 201-202.

Even the split between the largest Communist countries represents danger as well as opportunity. It means that henceforth the West will confront not alternating periods of hostility and conciliation but both at the same time. It can also happen that the two Communist giants may try to outbid each other in giving so-called liberation movements an anti-Western cast—the situation in the Congo is a good example.

The Troubled Partnership, p. 204.

The eagerness of many in the West to emphasize the liberalizing implications of Soviet economic trends and to make favorable interpretation of Soviet intentions a test of good faith may have the paradoxical consequence of strengthening the Soviet hard-liners. Soviet troops had hardly arrived in Prague when some Western leaders began to insist that the invasion would not affect the quest for détente while others continued to indicate a nostalgia for high-level meetings. Such an attitude hardly serves the cause of peace. The risk is great that if there is no penalty for intransigence there is no incentive for conciliation. The Kremlin may use negotiations—including arms control—as a safety valve to dissipate Western suspicions rather than as a serious endeavor to resolve concrete disputes or to remove the scourge of nuclear war.

If we focus our policy discussions on Soviet purposes, we confuse the debate in two ways: Soviet trends are too ambiguous to offer a reliable guide—it is possible that not even Soviet leaders fully understand the dynamics of their system; it deflects us from articulating the purposes we should pursue, whatever Soviet intentions. Peace will not, in any event, result from one grand settlement but from a long diplomatic process, and this process requires some clarity as to our destination. Confusing foreign policy with psychotherapy deprives us of criteria by which to judge the political foundations of international order. . . .

. . . . we should not again confuse a change of tone with a change of heart. We should not pose false inconsistencies between allied unity and détente; indeed, a true relaxation of tensions presupposes Western unity. We should concentrate negotiations on the concrete issues that threaten peace, such as intervention in the third world. Moderating the arms race must also be high on the agenda. None of this is possible without a concrete idea of what we understand by peace and a creative world order.

American Foreign Policy, pp. 88-90.

It should be obvious . . . that the Soviet domestic situation is complex and its relationship to foreign policy far from obvious. It is true that the risks of general nuclear war should be as unacceptable to Moscow as to Washington; but this truism does not automatically produce détente. It also seems to lessen the risks involved in local intervention. No doubt the current generation of Communist leaders lacks the ideological dynamism of their predecessors who made the revolution; at the same time, they have at their disposal a military machine of unprecedented strength, and they must deal with a bureaucracy of formidable vested interests. Unquestionably, Soviet consumers press their leaders to satisfy their demands; but it is equally true that an expanding modern economy is able to supply *both* guns and butter. Some Soviet leaders may have become more pragmatic; but in an elaborated Communist state, the results of pragmatism are complex. Once power is seized and industrialization is largely accomplished, the Communist Party faces a difficult situation. It is not needed to conduct the government, and it has no real function in running the economy (though it tries to do both). In order to justify its continued existence and command, it may develop a vested interest in vigilance against outside danger and thus in perpetuating a fairly high level of tension.

It is beyond the scope of this essay to go into detail on the issue of internal Communist evolution. But it may be appropriate to inquire why, in the past, every period of détente has proved stillborn. There have been at least five periods of peaceful coexistence since the Bolshevik seizure of power, one in each decade of the Soviet state. Each was hailed in the West as ushering in a new era of reconciliation and as signifying the long-awaited final change in Soviet purposes. Each ended abruptly with a new period of intransigence, which was generally ascribed to a victory of Soviet hard-liners rather than to the dynamics of the system. There were undoubtedly many reasons for this. But the tendency of many in the West to be content with changes of Soviet tone and to confuse atmosphere with substance surely did not help matters. It has enabled the Communist leaders to postpone the choice which they must make sooner or later: whether to use détente as a device to lull the West or whether to move toward a resolution of the outstanding differences. As long as this choice is postponed, the possibility exists that latent crises may run away with the principal protagonists, as happened in the Middle East and perhaps even in Czechoslovakia.

American Foreign Policy, pp. 87-88.

To break the pattern of the postwar period required policies that distinguished between the sources of conflict and their external or temporary manifestations. We needed not merely a better climate for our relations, but a new environment in which the United States and the Soviet Union could exercise their special responsibilities for peace. Ultimately we hoped to create mutual interests in maintaining and developing an international structure based on self-restraint in the pursuit of national interests.

The approach we adopted reflected certain general concepts.

—It was no longer realistic to allow Soviet-American relations to be predetermined by ideology. We had to recognize, of course, that many basic Soviet values would remain inimical to ours. Both sides had to accept the fact that neither was likely to persuade the other through polemical debates. But ideological elements did not preclude serious consideration of disputed issues.

—Irrespective of ideology, any relationship between two great powers would be highly competitive. Both sides had to recognize, however, that in this continuing competition there would be no permanent victor, and, equally important, that to focus one's own policy on attempts to gain advantages at the other's expense, could only aggravate tensions and precipitate counteractions.

—Both sides had to accept the fact that our differences could not be hidden merely by expressions of goodwill; they could only be resolved by precise solutions of major issues.

—Both sides had to understand that issues were interrelated: we could not effectively reduce tensions through marginal agreements or even an isolated agreement of importance. Experience had shown that isolated accomplishments were likely to fall victim to tensions and crises in other aspects of the relationship. Thus, if we were to achieve more than a superficial change, we had to address a broad range of issues.

—Finally, we would judge Soviet actions rather than words. The basic criterion would be a willingness to act with restraint. We would respond constructively to Soviet initiatives; progress in one area would help maintain momentum in other negotiations. We would also make it clear that aggressive behavior could imperil our entire relationship. By linking all aspects of Soviet-American relations, we could hope that progress, if it came, could lead to a broadly based understanding about international conduct.

U.S. Foreign Policy for the 1970's, pp. 27-28.

On this basis we have succeeded in transforming U.S.-Soviet relations in many important ways. Our two countries have concluded a historic accord to limit strategic arms. We have substantially reduced the risk of direct U.S.-Soviet confrontation in crisis areas. The problem of Berlin has been resolved by negotiation. We and our allies have engaged the Soviet Union in negotiations on major issues of European security, including a reduction of military forces in central Europe. We have reached a series of bilateral agreements on cooperation—health, environment, space, science and technology, as well as trade. These accords are designed to create a vested interest in cooperation and restraint.

Pacem in Terris Speech, p. 528.

Détente is founded on a frank recognition of basic differences and dangers. Precisely because we are conscious that these differences exist, we have sought to channel our relations with the U.S.S.R. into a more stable framework—a structure of interrelated and interdependent agreements. Forward movement in our relations must be on a broad front, encompassing a wide range of mutually reinforcing activities, so that groups and individuals in both countries will have a vested interest in the maintenance of peace and the growth of a stable international order.

Since détente is rooted in a recognition of differences and based on the prevention of disaster, there are sharp limits to what we can insist upon as part of this relationship. We have a right to demand responsible international behavior from the U.S.S.R.; we did not hesitate to make this clear during the Middle East crisis. We also have a right to demand that agreements we sign are observed in good faith.

But with respect to basic changes in the Soviet system, the issue is not whether we condone what the U.S.S.R. does internally; it is whether and to what extent we can risk other objectives—and especially the building of a structure for peace—for these domestic changes. I believe that we cannot and that to do so would obscure, and in the long run defeat, what must remain our overriding objective: the prevention of nuclear war.

Statement to Senate Finance
Committee, p. 323.

The administration [early] took the view—which it has never abandoned—that intensified trade should grow out of a generally improved relationship; in short, that our relations with the U.S.S.R. should proceed on a broad front. . . .

. . . It was only after the 1972 summit that the President determined that trade could reasonably be expanded. By that time we were on the way to a Viet-Nam settlement, Berlin had been the subject of a major formal agreement, the first SALT [Strategic Arms Limitation Talks] agreements had been completed, a set of principles setting standards for U.S.-Soviet relations had been signed at the summit, a series of bilateral cooperation agreements in a wide field of activities had been signed and were in process of implementation. In sum, both in substance and tone the U.S.-Soviet relationship had undergone significant change and a process of normalization committing the top leaders on both sides had been initiated. In this setting, the gradual transformation of trading relationships was a logical step that could serve to provide additional incentives for maintaining the course which both sides had set for themselves. . . .

Thus, the major impact of the continued denial of MFN status to the Soviet Union would be political, not economic. MFN was withdrawn in 1951, largely as a political act. Our unwillingness to remove this discrimination now would call into question our intent to move toward an improved relationship. It would jeopardize a moderate evolution in all areas, including the Middle East. It would prevent the implementation of the U.S.-Soviet Trade Agreement, as well as the lend-lease accord—involving repayment of over $700 million to the United States.

Statement to Senate Finance
Committee, p. 324.

A number of factors have produced this change in the international environment. By the end of the sixties and the beginning of the seventies the time was propitious—no matter what administration was in office in the United States—for a major attempt to improve

U.S.-Soviet relations. Contradictory tendencies contested for pre-eminence in Soviet policy; events could have tipped the scales toward either increased aggressiveness or toward conciliation.

—The fragmentation in the Communist world in the 1960's challenged the leading position of the U.S.S.R. and its claim to be the arbiter of orthodoxy. The U.S.S.R. could have reacted by adopting a more aggressive attitude toward the capitalist world in order to assert its militant vigilance; instead, the changing situation and U.S. policy seem to have encouraged Soviet leaders to cooperate in at least a temporary lessening of tension with the West.

—The prospect of achieving a military position of near parity with the United States in strategic forces could have tempted Moscow to use its expanding military capability to strive more determinedly for expansion; in fact, it tempered the militancy of some of its action and sought to stabilize at least some aspects of the military competition through negotiations.

—The very real economic problems of the U.S.S.R. and Eastern Europe could have reinforced autarkic policies and the tendency to create a closed system; in actuality, the Soviet Union and its allies have come closer to acknowledging the reality of an interdependent world economy.

—Finally, when faced with the hopes of its own people for greater well-being, the Soviet Government could have continued to stimulate the suspicions of the cold war to further isolate Soviet society: in fact, it chose—however inadequately and slowly—to seek to calm its public opinion by joining in a relaxation of tensions.

Statement to Senate Foreign Relations
Committee, p. 507.

Over time, trade and investment may leaven the autarkic tendencies of the Soviet system, invite gradual association of the Soviet economy with the world economy, and foster a degree of interdependence that adds an element of stability to the political equation.

Statement to Senate Foreign Relations
Committee, p. 512.

9. Summitry and Personal Diplomacy

When the Paris summit meetings collapsed, a sudden reversal took place in the West. . . . Personal diplomacy, which had been thought capable of ending the Cold War, was now held responsible for perpetuating it. As Mr. Khrushchev's mood changed, the West seemed as much in danger of being mesmerized by his frown as it had earlier been beguiled by his smile.

The Necessity for Choice, p. 180.

The temptation to conduct personal diplomacy derives from the notion of peace prevalent in both the United States and Great Britain. If peace is the "normal" relation among states, it follows that tensions must be caused by shortsightedness or misunderstanding and that they can be removed by a change of heart of the leading statesmen. President Eisenhower, before embarking on an unprecedented round of visits to foreign capitals, was at pains to insist that his purpose was to "clear" the atmosphere rather than to negotiate. If peace ultimately depends on personalities, abstract good will may well seem more important than a concrete program. Indeed, the attempt to achieve specific settlements can appear as an obstacle rather than as an aid to peace.

The Necessity for Choice, p. 181.

. . . . One wonders, however, whether the democracies' notion of normality is not their Achilles' heel. An atmosphere of confidence is undoubtedly helpful. It is less certain, however, whether the free countries render themselves or the cause of peace a service by making a settlement seem so simple and by evading all difficult issues. Had the Cold War really resulted from personal distrust or were the causes deeper? Was the tension caused by the intransigence of the Soviet tone or the intransigence of Soviet acts? Is it not possible that the yearning for agreement . . . and the identification of a settlement with good personal relations are themselves obstacles to serious negotiation? What conceivable incentive could be left for the Soviet leaders to negotiate responsibly at a summit when the mere fact of its being assembled plays so large a role in Western thinking?

The Necessity for Choice, p. 183-184.

. . . many of the arguments advanced on behalf of summit diplomacy were fatuous in the extreme. It was urged that only the heads of state could settle the really intractable disputes. No subordinate, it was said, would dare to abandon the rigid positions of the Cold War. In the Soviet Union, in particular, only Mr. Khrushchev was in a position to make really fundamental decisions. And the mere fact that a summit meeting was in prospect was thought to place constraints on Soviet intransigence. A series of summit meetings, according to this line of argument, could not fail to relieve tensions.

Many of these contentions were open to serious doubt even before the collapse of the Paris Conference. It is trivial to pretend that problems of the complexity of those which have rent the world for a decade and a half can be solved in a few days by harassed men meeting in the full light of publicity. It cannot be in the interest of the democracies to adopt a style of diplomacy which places such a premium on the authority of a few leaders. Mr. Khrushchev may be the supreme ruler in the Soviet Union and the only one with sufficient power to make binding agreements. It does not follow that the democracies can coexist with a dictatorship only by imitating its method of operation.

The Necessity for Choice, pp. 185-186.

. . . . When heads of state are the principal negotiators, their most effective bargaining device—in some circumstances the only available one—is to stake their prestige in a manner which makes any concession appear as an intolerable loss of face.

The evasion of concreteness, the reliance on personalities, the implication that all problems can be settled with one grand gesture, all these tempt the Soviet leaders to use negotiations to demoralize the West. It is in the Soviet interest to turn all disputes into clashes of personalities. The peoples of the free world cannot be expected to run risks or to make exertions because of a personal dispute.

The Necessity for Choice, p. 187.

The advantage of a summit meeting is that the participants possess the authority to settle disputes. The disadvantage is that they cannot be disavowed. A summit conference can make binding decisions more rapidly than any other diplomatic forum. By the same token, the disagreements are liable to be more intractable and the decisions more irrevocable. The possibility of using summit conferences to mark a new departure in the relations of states should not be underestimated. At the same time, it would be foolish to deny the perils of having as principal negotiators the men who make the final decision about the use of hydrogen bombs. Frustration or humiliation may cause them to embark on an irrevocable course. A summit conference may contribute to clarification of the opposing points of view. But this is helpful only if the original tension was caused by misunderstanding. Otherwise, clarifying the opposing points of view may only deepen the schism. In short, the same factors which make for speed of decision also increase the risks of disagreement.

Moreover, when heads of state become the principal negotiators, they may soon find themselves so preoccupied with the process of bargaining that they have little time or energy available for formulating policy.[13] In the ambulatory diplomacy, preceding the Paris summit conference, it was an oddity when all heads of state were at home simultaneously. During his last two years in office President Eisenhower was at conferences, preparing for or recuperating from good will visits almost constantly. Such a diplomacy may suit a dictatorship or a state which wishes to demoralize its opponents by confusing all issues. It is not conducive to developing constructive long-range policies. It is a useful device to buy time, though at a price which makes it unlikely that the time will be well used.

In such an atmosphere, agreement all too often becomes an end in itself. However unimportant the settlement, no matter how irrelevant, it is said to contribute to a climate of confidence which will "improve" the situation.

The Necessity for Choice, pp. 188-189.

Whether or not to resort to summit meetings is essentially a practical and not a moral issue. They should be held only when there is some clear, substantive advantage in prospect. It is sometimes easier for heads of state to break a deadlock and to chart a new course than it is for their subordinates, who are inevitably committed to existing policies. High-level meetings can ratify agreements and give general guidelines for further detailed negotiations. They should be used for these purposes with courage and conviction. But to see in them a magic solvent for all difficulties is to build policy on illusion. Such a course creates constant temptations for the Soviet leaders to use meetings of heads of state to demoralize the West. Phrases such as "relaxation of tensions" and "peaceful coexistence" become devices to press extreme demands. The West is invited to accept Soviet proposals or suffer the penalty of a return to the vilifications of the Cold War.

When the primary purpose of summit meetings is thought to be the fostering of abstract good will, they become not a forum for negotiations but a substitute for them; not an expression of a policy

---

[13] For a brilliant discussion of the problem posed by summit diplomacy for the American presidency, see Dean Rusk, "The President," *Foreign Affairs*, April 1960, pp. 353-369.

but a means of obscuring its absence. The constant international travels of heads of government without a clear program or purpose may be less an expression of statesmanship than a symptom of panic.

The Necessity for Choice, pp. 190-191.

Belief in the predominance of "objective" factors explains why Soviet leaders, whenever they have had to make a choice between Western goodwill and a territorial or political gain, have unhesitatingly chosen the latter. The friendship of the West built up during the heroic efforts of World War II was ruthlessly sacrificed to the possibility of establishing Communist-controlled governments in Eastern Europe. The spirit of Geneva did not survive the temptations offered by the prospect of penetrating the Middle East. The spirit of Camp David ended with another ultimatum on Berlin. The many overtures of the Kennedy Administration were rebuffed until the Cuban missile crisis demonstrated that the balance of forces was not in fact favorable.

The Soviet reliance on "objective" factors is one of the reasons that negotiations with the Soviets have often been so frustrating. Communist negotiators cannot admit that they could be swayed by the arguments of opponents whose understanding of the basic laws of historical development is, by definition, inferior to their own. They cannot reciprocate "concessions" because they believe that concessions are made to reality, not to individuals. They may change their position, but they will go to great lengths to demonstrate that they did so of their own volition and at their own pace. For them a great deal depends on avoiding what seems basic to most Western negotiators: the give-and-take of a bargaining process. Their attitude toward Western negotiators is very similar to that of Western psychiatrists toward their patients: no matter what is said, they think that they understand their Western counterpart better than he understands himself. This is one of the reasons that exercises in personal diplomacy—even at the highest level—have been so futile. No Soviet leader could make an agreement based on the proposition that he has been impressed by the personal qualities of a capitalist statesman. Settlements are possible; but to be meaningful in Soviet eyes they must reflect "objective" conditions and not a personal relationship.

The Troubled Partnership, pp. 197-198.

Domestic considerations impel many Western leaders to present themselves to their electorate as the architects of a lasting peace.

The temptation is, therefore, strong to treat a more conciliatory Communist tone as a permanent conversion to a peaceful course and to gear everything to personal diplomacy.

Such attitudes will cause the West to squander its opportunities, as has happened so often in the past. The prospects for peace are not served by leaving the Soviet leadership with the impression that any action, no matter how belligerent, can always be reversed by a change of tone. Negotiations will prove empty if they are confined to vague protestations of goodwill. If a detente is not to be part of another cycle leading to renewed tensions, it is essential that negotiations be concrete and programs specific.

The Troubled Partnership, p. 203.

If the West is to act purposefully in this situation, it must develop a common policy and a specific program. The temptation for bilateral approaches is great. Each national leader, depending on his temperament, has visions of appearing as the arbiter of a final settlement or of adding Communist pressures to his own as a bargaining device within the Alliance. This sets up a vicious circle. Since leaders generally do not reach eminence without a touch of vanity and since some stake their prestige on their ability to woo their Soviet counterparts, they tend to present their contacts with the Soviets as a considerable accomplishment. But the real issues have gone unresolved because they are genuinely difficult; hence they are usually avoided during summit diplomacy in favor of showy but essentially peripheral gestures. The vaguer the East-West discourse, the greater will be the confusion in the West. Moreover, each leader faces two different audiences: toward his own people he will be tempted to leave the impression that he has made a unique contribution to peace; toward his allies he will be forced to insist that he will make no settlement in which they do not participate. Excessive claims are coupled with reassurances to uneasy allies which are in turn tempted to pursue bilateral diplomacy.

Such a course is suicidal for the West.

The Troubled Partnership, pp. 205-206.

10. Détente

There is no doubt that the avoidance of war must be a primary goal of all responsible statesmen. The desirability of maintaining peace cannot be the subject of either intellectual or partisan political controversy in the free world. The only reasonable issue is how best to achieve this objective.

And here there is reason for serious concern. A welter of slogans fills the air. "Relaxation of tensions," "flexibility," "new approaches," "negotiable proposals," are variously put forth, as remedies to the impasse of the Cold War. But the programs to give these phrases meaning have proved much more difficult to define. The impression has been created that the missing ingredient has been a "willingness to negotiate." While this criticism is correct for some periods, particularly John Foster Dulles' incumbency as Secretary of State, it is not a just comment when applied to the entire post-war era. Hardly a year has passed without at least some negotiation with the Communist countries. There have been six Foreign Ministers' Conferences and three summit meetings. Periods of intransigence have alternated with spasmodic efforts to settle all problems at one fell swoop. The abortive summit meeting of 1960 proved that tensions have sometimes been increased as much by the manner in which diplomacy has been conducted as by the refusal to negotiate. The Cold War has been perpetuated not only by the abdication of diplomacy but also by its emptiness and sterility.

What, then, has made the conduct of diplomacy so difficult? Why have tensions continued whether we negotiated or failed to negotiate? There are four basic causes: (1) the destructiveness of modern weapons, (2) the polarization of power in the contemporary period, (3) the nature of the conflict, (4) national attitudes peculiar to the West and particularly to the United States.

The Necessity for Choice, pp. 169-170.

The inherent tensions of a two-power world are compounded by the clash of opposing ideologies. For over a generation now the Communist leaders have proclaimed their devotion to the overthrow of the capitalist world. They have insisted that the economic system of their opponents was based on exploitation and war. They have never wavered from asserting the inevitability or the crucial importance of their triumph. To be sure, periods of peaceful coexistence have alternated with belligerence, particularly since the advent of Mr. Khrushchev. But one of the principal Communist justifications for a *détente* can hardly prove very reassuring to the free world; peace is advocated not for its own sake but because the West is said to have grown so weak that it will go to perdition without a last convulsive upheaval.   *The Necessity for Choice*, p. 172.

Finally, relations with the Communist world have changed dramatically since the Cuban missile crisis. Most of our European Allies have reached the conclusion that the two main nuclear powers will avoid a direct military confrontation for an indefinite period. This conviction has been strengthened by the hope of some, and the suspicion of others, that bilateral United States-Soviet dealings are under way. Such an atmosphere of detente removes the previous urgency for Allied cohesion. As the Soviet threat appears to recede, the scope for largely national action widens proportionately. As the impression grows that bilateral Soviet-United States negotiations are proceeding, Third Force tendencies in Europe are stimulated. This issue is not whether the United States would make a "deal" contrary to the interests of its Allies. It is rather than in an alliance of sovereign states each country will think that it is a better judge of its own requirements than any partner, however close. No ally will be prepared to let another negotiate about what it considers its vital interests.

As the detente develops, the need to transform the Alliance from its present defensive concept into a political arrangement defining itself by some positive goals will grow ever more urgent. Defense against a military threat will soon lose its force as a political bond. Negotiations with the East will prove corrosive unless they go hand in hand with the creation of common political purposes and the institutions to embody them. The need, in short, is to go from alliance to community.

The Troubled Partnership, pp. 9-10.

Peace offensives, of course, are not new in Soviet history. Peaceful co-existence has been avowed since the advent of Communism in Russia. It was stressed particularly between 1924–1939; between 1941–1946; at the time of the Geneva Summit Conference of 1955; again on the occasion of Khrushchev's visit to the United States in 1959; and following the Cuban missile crisis in 1962. On each occasion the reason for the detente was some internal or external strain on the Soviet system. In 1924, it was the struggle between Stalin and Trotsky, which was followed by the forced collectivization of agriculture and the purges; in 1941–1946 it was the German invasion; in 1955 it was the succession struggle after the death of Stalin; in 1959 it was part of a Soviet attempt to push the Allies out of Berlin; since 1962 it has been caused by the shock of the defeat in Cuba and the internal strains on the Soviet system.

On each occasion the period of relaxation ended when an opportunity for expanding Communism presented itself. The period of tranquillity after 1924 was followed by the annexation of Bessarabia, the Baltic States and one third of Poland, as well as an attack on Finland. World War II led to the creation of the satellite orbit in Eastern Europe. The spirit of Geneva gave way to an attempted penetration of the Middle East and a crisis over Berlin. And, the spirit of Camp David was succeeded by another Berlin crisis which did not end until the installation of Soviet missiles in Cuba.

During each previous Soviet peace offensive, many in the West— including some who thought of themselves as staunchly, sometimes almost religiously, anti-Communist—hailed a fundamental change in Soviet attitude. This demonstrates the extent of the American consensus that conflict is usually the result of individual malice rather than of structural causes. The corollary is that East-West tensions can be ended by a simple change of heart on the part of Communist leaders.

The Troubled Partnership, pp. 192-193.

. . . peaceful co-existence is never advocated for its own sake. It is justified primarily as a tactical device to overthrow the West at minimum risk.

The Troubled Partnership, p. 198.

All of this suggests that the current period of relaxation of tension has been initiated by the Soviets not because a few individuals have overcome the opposition of some unnamed Stalinists, but because conditions require it. To the West the challenge presented by this detente can be defined as follows: When the Communist world faces internal difficulties, should we bask in the relative calm of the Communist tone, or should we use the opportunity to press for the settlement of issues that produced the tension in the first place?

The Troubled Partnership, p. 203.

Our policy with respect to détente is clear: We shall resist aggressive foreign policies. Détente cannot survive irresponsibility in any area, including the Middle East. As for the internal policies of closed systems, the United States will never forget that the antagonism between freedom and its enemies is part of the reality of the modern age. We are not neutral in that struggle. As long as we remain powerful, we will use our influence to promote freedom, as we always have.

Pacem in Terris Speech, p. 529.

Détente is an imperative. In a world shadowed by the danger of nuclear holocaust, there is no rational alternative to the pursuit of relaxation of tensions. But we must take care that the pursuit of détente not undermine the friendships which made détente possible.

Pilgrims of Great Britain Speech, p. 779.

Let us remember that we seek détente with the Soviet Union for one overwhelming reason: Both countries have the capability to destroy each other—and most of the rest of the world in the process. Thus, both of us have an overriding obligation to do all in our power to prevent such a catastrophe.

Détente is not rooted in agreement on values; it becomes above all necessary because each side recognizes that the other is a potential adversary in a nuclear war. To us, détente is a process of managing relations with a potentially hostile country in order to preserve peace while maintaining our vital interests. In a nuclear age, this is in itself an objective not without moral validity—it may indeed be the most profound imperative of all.

Statement to Senate Finance
Committee, p. 323.

Some fundamental principles guide this policy:

The United States cannot base its policy solely on Moscow's good intentions. But neither can we insist that all forward movement must await a convergence of American and Soviet purposes. We seek, regardless of Soviet intentions, to serve peace through a systematic resistance to pressure and conciliatory responses to moderate behavior.

We must oppose aggressive actions and irresponsible behavior. But we must not seek confrontations lightly.

We must maintain a strong national defense while recognizing that in the nuclear age the relationship between military strength and politically usable power is the most complex in all history.

Where the age-old antagonism between freedom and tyranny is concerned, we are not neutral. But other imperatives impose limits on our ability to produce internal changes in foreign countries. Consciousness of our limits is recognition of the necessity of peace—not moral callousness. The preservation of human life and human society are moral values, too.

We must be mature enough to recognize that to be stable a relationship must provide advantages to both sides and that the most constructive international relationships are those in which both parties perceive an element of gain. Moscow will benefit from certain measures, just as we will from others. The balance cannot be struck on each issue every day, but only over the whole range of relations and over a period of time.

Statement to Senate Foreign Relations
Committee, p. 506.

. . . . If détente can be justified only by a basic change in Soviet motivation, the temptation becomes overwhelming to base U.S.-Soviet relations not on realistic appraisal but on tenuous hopes: a change in Soviet tone is taken as a sign of a basic change of philosophy. Atmosphere is confused with substance. Policy oscillates between poles of suspicion and euphoria.

Neither extreme is realistic, and both are dangerous. The hopeful view ignores that we and the Soviets are bound to compete for the foreseeable future. The pessimistic view ignores that we have some parallel interests and that we are compelled to coexist. Détente encourages an environment in which competitors can regulate and restrain their differences and ultimately move from competition to cooperation.

Statement to Senate Foreign Relations
Committee, p. 507.

We sought to explore every avenue toward an honorable and just accommodation while remaining determined not to settle for mere atmospherics. We relied on a balance of mutual interests rather than Soviet intentions. When challenged—such as in the Middle East, the Caribbean, or Berlin—we always responded firmly. And when Soviet policy moved toward conciliation, we sought to turn what may have started as a tactical maneuver into a durable pattern of conduct.

Our approach proceeds from the conviction that, in moving forward across a wide spectrum of negotiations, progress in one area adds momentum to progress in other areas. If we succeed, then no agreement stands alone as an isolated accomplishment vulnerable to the next crisis. We did not invent the interrelationship between issues expressed in the so-called linkage concept; it was a reality because of the range of problems and areas in which the interests of the United States and the Soviet Union impinge on each other. We have looked for progress in a series of agreements settling specific political issues, and we have sought to relate these to a new standard of international conduct appropriate to the dangers of the nuclear age. By acquiring a stake in this network of relationships with the West, the Soviet Union may become more conscious of what it would lose by a return to confrontation. Indeed, it is our hope that it will develop a self-interest in fostering the entire process of relaxation of tensions. . . .

Détente is all the more important because of what the creation of a new set of international relations demands of us with respect to other countries and areas. President Ford has assigned the highest priority to maintaining the vitality of our partnerships in Europe, Asia, and Latin America. Our security ties with our allies are essential, but we also believe that recognition of the interdependence of the contemporary world requires cooperation in many other fields. Cooperation becomes more difficult if the United States is perceived by allied public opinion as an obstacle to peace and if public debate is polarized on the issue of whether friendship with the United States is inconsistent with East-West reconciliation.

Statement to Senate Foreign Relations
Committee, p. 508.

We demonstrated then, and stand ready to do so again, that America will not yield to pressure or the threat of force. We made clear then, as we do today, that détente cannot be pursued selectively in one area or toward one group of countries only. For us détente is indivisible.

Statement to Senate Foreign Relations
Committee, p. 509.

Détente is admittedly far from a modern equivalent to the kind of stable peace that characterized most of the 19th century. But it is a long step away from the bitter and aggressive spirit that has characterized so much of the postwar period. When linked to such broad and unprecedented projects as SALT, détente takes on added meaning and opens prospects of a more stable peace. . . .

To be sure, the process of détente raises serious issues for many people. Let me deal with these in terms of the principles which underlie our policy.

First, if détente is to endure, both sides must benefit.

There is no question that the Soviet Union obtains benefits from détente. On what other grounds would the tough-minded members of the Politburo sustain it? But the essential point surely must be that détente serves American and world interests as well. If these coincide with some Soviet interests, this will only strengthen the durability of the process.

On the global scale, in terms of the conventional measures of power, influence, and position, our interests have not suffered—they have generally prospered. In many areas of the world, the influence and the respect we enjoy are greater than was the case for many years.

It is also true that Soviet influence and presence are felt in many parts of the world. But this is a reality that would exist without détente. The record shows that détente does not deny us the opportunity to react to it and to offset it. . . .

Second, building a new relationship with the Soviet Union does not entail any devaluation of traditional alliance relations.

Our approach to relations with the U.S.S.R. has always been, and will continue to be, rooted in the belief that the cohesion of our alliances, and particularly the Atlantic alliance, is a precondition to establishing a more constructive relationship with the U.S.S.R. . . .

Third, the emergence of more normal relations with the Soviet Union must not undermine our resolve to maintain our national defense.

There is a tendency in democratic societies to relax as dangers seem to recede; there is an inclination to view the maintenance of strength as incompatible with relaxation of tensions rather than its precondition. But this is primarily a question of leadership. We shall attempt to be vigilant to the dangers facing America. This administration will not be misled—or mislead—on issues of national defense. At the same time, we do not accept the proposition that we need crises to sustain our defense. A society that needs artificial crises to do what is needed for survival will soon find itself in mortal danger.

Fourth, we must know what can and cannot be achieved in changing human conditions in the East.

The question of dealing with Communist governments has troubled the American people and the Congress since 1917. There has always been a fear that by working with a government whose internal policies differ so sharply with our own we are in some manner condoning these policies or encouraging their continuation. Some argue that until there is a genuine "liberalization"—or signs of serious progress in this direction—all elements of conciliation in Soviet policy must be regarded as temporary and tactical. In that view, demands for internal changes must be the precondition for the pursuit of a relaxation of tensions with the Soviet Union.

Our view is different. We shall insist on responsible international behavior by the Soviet Union and use it as the primary index of our relationship. Beyond this we will use our influence to the maximum to alleviate suffering and to respond to humane appeals. We know what we stand for, and we shall leave no doubt about it.

Statement to Senate Foreign Relations
Committee, pp. 515-518.

Détente is a process, not a permanent achievement. The agenda is full and continuing. Obviously the main concern must be to reduce the sources of potential conflict. This requires efforts in several inter-related areas:

—The military competition in all its aspects must be subject to increasingly firm restraints by both sides.

—Political competition, especially in moments of crisis, must be guided by the principles of restraint set forth in the documents described earlier. Crises there will be, but the United States and the Soviet Union have a special obligation deriving from the unimaginable military power that they wield and represent. Exploitation of crisis situations for unilateral gain is not acceptable.

—Restraint in crises must be augmented by cooperation in removing the causes of crises. There have been too many instances, notably in the Middle East, which demonstrate that policies of unilateral advantage sooner or later run out of control and lead to the brink of war, if not beyond.

—The process of negotiations and consultation must be continuous and intense. But no agreement between the nuclear superpowers can be durable if made over the heads of other nations which have a stake in the outcome. We should not seek to impose peace; we can, however, see that our own actions and conduct are conducive to peace.

Statement to Senate Foreign Relations
Committee, p. 518.

We must assess not only individual challenges to détente but also their cumulative impact:

If we justify each agreement with Moscow only when we can show unilateral gain,

If we strive for an elusive strategic "superiority,"

If we systematically block benefits to the Soviet Union,

If we try to transform the Soviet system by pressure,

If in short, we look for final results before we agree to any results, then we would be reviving the doctrines of liberation and massive retaliation of the 1950's. And we would do so at a time when Soviet physical power and influence on the world are greater than a quarter century ago when those policies were devised and failed. The futility of such a course is as certain as its danger.

Let there be no question, however, that Soviet actions could destroy détente as well:

If the Soviet Union uses détente to strengthen its military capacity in all fields,

If in crises it acts to sharpen tension,

If it does not contribute to progress toward stability,

If it seeks to undermine our alliances,

If it is deaf to the urgent needs of the least developed and the emerging issues of interdependence, then it in turn tempts a return to the tensions and conflicts we have made such efforts to overcome. The policy of confrontation has worked for neither of the superpowers.

We have insisted toward the Soviet Union that we cannot have the atmosphere of détente without the substance. It is equally clear that the substance of détente will disappear in an atmosphere of hostility.

Statement to Senate Foreign Relations
Committee, p. 519.

11. Bureaucracy, Creativity, and the Statesman

It can never be the task of leadership to solicit a consensus, but to create the conditions which will make a consensus possible. A leader, if he performs his true function, must resign himself to being alone part of the time, at least while he charts the road.

"American Policy and Preventive War," p. 336.

What then is the role of statesmanship? A scholarship of social determinism has reduced the statesman to a lever on a machine called "history," to the agent of a fate which he may dimly discern but which he accomplishes regardless of his will. And this belief in the pervasiveness of circumstance and the impotence of the individual extends to the notion of policy-making. One hears a great deal about the contingency of planning because of the unavailability of fact, about the difficulty of action because of the limitation of knowledge. It cannot be denied, of course, that policy does not occur in a void, that the statesman is confronted with material he must treat as given. Not only geography and the availability of resources trace the limits of statesmanship, but also the character of the people and the nature of its historical experience. But to say that policy does not create its own substance is not the same as saying that the substance is self-implementing. . . .

The test of a statesman, then, is his ability to recognize the real relationship of forces and to make this knowledge serve his ends. . . .

. . . it is not sufficient to judge the statesman by his conceptions alone, for unlike the philosopher he must implement his vision. And the statesman is inevitably confronted by the inertia of his material, by the fact that other powers are not factors to be manipulated but forces to be reconciled; that the requirements of security differ with the geographic location and the domestic structure of the powers. His instrument is diplomacy, the art of relating states to each other by agreement rather than by the exercise of force, by the representation of a ground of action which reconciles particular aspirations with a general consensus. Because diplomacy depends on persuasion and not imposition, it presupposes a determinate framework, either through an agreement on a legitimizing principle or, theoretically, through an identical interpretation of power-relationships, although the latter is in practice the most difficult to attain. . . .

The acid test of a policy, however, is its ability to obtain domestic support. This has two aspects: the problem of legitimizing a policy *within* the governmental apparatus, which is a problem of bureaucratic rationality; and that of harmonizing it with the national experience, which is a problem of historical development. . . . For the spirit of policy and that of bureaucracy are diametrically opposed. The essence of policy is its contingency; its success depends on the correctness of an estimate which is in part conjectural. The essence of bureaucracy is its quest for safety; its success is calculability. Profound policy thrives on perpetual creation, on a constant redefinition of goals. Good administration thrives on routine, the definition of relationships which can survive mediocrity. Policy involves an adjustment of risks; administration an avoidance of deviation. Policy justifies itself by the relationship of its measures and its sense of proportion; administration by the rationality of each action in terms of a given goal. The attempt to conduct policy bureaucratically leads to a quest for calculability which tends to become a prisoner of events. The effort to administer politically leads to total irresponsibility, because bureaucracies are designed to execute, not to conceive.

The temptation to conduct policy administratively is ever present, because most governments are organized primarily for the conduct of domestic policy, whose chief problem is the implementation of social decisions, a task which is limited only by its technical feasibility. But the concern with technical problems in foreign affairs leads to a standard which evaluates by mistakes avoided rather than by goals achieved, and to a belief that ability is more likely to be judged by the pre-vision of catastrophes than the discovery of opportunities. . . .

For this reason, too, it is dangerous to separate planning from the responsibility of execution. For responsibility involves a standard of judgment, a legitimacy. But the standard of a bureaucracy is different

from that of the social effort. Social goals are justified by the legitimizing principle of the domestic structure, which may be rationality,
tradition or charisma, but which is in any case considered an *ultimate*
value. Bureaucratic measures are justified by an essentially *instru-
mental* standard, the suitability of certain actions for achieving ends
conceived as given. A society is capable of only a limited range of
decisions, because its values are relatively fixed; an ideal bureaucracy
should be able to carry out *any* decision which is administratively
feasible. The attempt to define social goals bureaucratically will, therefore, always lead to the distortion inherent in applying a rationality
of means to the development of ends.

A World Restored, pp. 324-327.

The statesman is therefore like one of the heroes in classical
drama who has had a vision of the future but who cannot transmit it
directly to his fellow-men and who cannot validate its "truth."
Nations learn only by experience; they "know" only when it is too
late to act. But statesmen must act *as if* their intuition were already
experience, as if their aspiration were truth. It is for this reason that
statesmen often share the fate of prophets, that they are without
honour in their own country, that they always have a difficult task in
legitimizing their programmes domestically, and that their greatness is
usually apparent only in retrospect when their intuition has become
experience. The statesman must therefore be an educator; he must
bridge the gap between a people's experience and his vision, between
a nation's tradition and its future. In this task his possibilities are
limited. A statesman who too far outruns the experience of his people
will fail in achieving a domestic consensus, however wise his policies;
witness Castlereagh. A statesman who limits his policy to the experience of his people will doom himself to sterility; witness Metternich.

It is for this reason that most great statesmen have been either
representatives of essentially conservative social structures or revolu-
tionaries: the conservative is effective because of his understanding
of the experience of his people and of the essence of a continuing
relationship, which is the key to a stable international organization.
And the revolutionary, because he transcends experience and identifies
the just with the possible. The conservative (particularly if he represents an essentially conservative social structure) is legitimized by a
consensus on the basic goals of the social effort and on the nature of
the social experience. There is, therefore, no need to justify every
step along the way. The revolutionary is legitimized by his charis-

matic quality, by an agreement on the legitimacy of his person or of his principle. His means are therefore considered incidental; his ends or his person legitimize the means. A conservative structure produces a notion of *quality*, which provides the framework of great conception; a revolutionary order produces a notion of exaltation, which dissolves technical limitations. Both thus deal with the fundamental problem of statesmanship: how to produce an understanding of the *complexity* of policy when it is impossible to produce a comprehension of its *substance*.

A World Restored, pp. 329-330.

Our dilemma is made more intractable because our foreign policy has been far too bi-partisan. Over the decade of the 1950's one looks in vain for any fundamental criticism of the main trends in American policy. Such criticism as has been offered was frequently tactical or *ex post facto.* The fatuous diplomacy which preceded the abortive summit meeting of 1960 in Paris went largely unchallenged until its failure became apparent. But the test of statesmanship is the adequacy of its evaluation *before* the event. A democracy, to be vital, requires leaders willing to stand alone.

The Necessity for Choice, p. 3.

Equally worrisome is our interpretation of the process in which we find ourselves engaged. Throughout a decade of almost continuous decline the notion that time was on our side has been at the basis of much of our policy. Our attitudes therefore have tended to remain passive. When history contains a guarantee of eventual success, survival can easily become the primary goal. Creativity, innovation, sacrifice pale before tactical considerations of dealing with day-to-day concerns. A powerful incentive exists for deferring difficult choices. It is not surprising, then, that our policies have lacked vitality and that public discussion has focused on symptoms, not causes. But it is equally clear that such attitudes doom us to sterility in a revolutionary period.

The Necessity for Choice, pp. 5-6.

Nothing is more important for America than to give up its illusions. Too much of our domestic debate gives the impression that we are working towards a static condition called peace. We sometimes argue as if only a single new initiative or one brilliant move stands between us and normalcy. Many of us seem to believe that we can dramatically sweep all before us in an atmosphere of universal approbation.

But even with the wisest policies we can expect nothing of the sort. Our generation will live in the midst of change. Our norm is the fact of upheaval. The success of our actions is not measured by short-term tranquillity. It is defined by whether we can shape the currents of our time in the light of our values. What is needed even more than different policies is a different style and a more dynamic attitude.

The Necessity for Choice, p. 7.

One of the paradoxes of an increasingly specialized, bureaucratized society is that the qualities rewarded in the rise to eminence are less and less the qualities required once eminence is reached. Specialization encourages administrative and technical skills, which are not necessarily those needed for leadership. Good administration depends on the ability to co-ordinate the specialized functions of a bureaucracy. The task of the executive is to infuse and occasionally to transcend routine with purpose. Administration is concerned with execution. Policymaking must address itself also to developing a sense of direction.

Yet, while the head of an organization requires a different outlook from that of his administrative subordinates, he must generally be recruited from their ranks. Eminence thus is often reached for reasons and according to criteria which are irrelevant to the tasks which must be performed in the highest positions. Despite all personnel procedures, and perhaps because of them, superior performance at the apex of an organization is frequently in the deepest sense accidental.

This problem, which exists in all complex societies, is especially characteristic of the United States. In a society that has prided itself on its "business" character, it is inevitable that the qualities which are most esteemed in civilian pursuits should also be generally rewarded by high public office. As a result, the typical Cabinet or sub-Cabinet officer in America comes either from business or from the legal profession. But very little in the experience that forms these men produces the combination of political acumen, conceptual skill, persuasive power, and substantive knowledge required for the highest positions of government.

... The executive's task is conceived as choosing among administrative proposals in the formulation of which he has no part and with the substance of which he is often unfamiliar. A premium is placed on "presentations" which take the least effort to grasp—in practice usually oral "briefing." (This accounts for the emergence of the specialist in "briefings" who prepares charts, one-page summaries, etc.) The result is that in our society the executive grows dependent to an increasing extent on his subordinates' conception of the essential elements of a problem.

In such an environment little opportunity exists for real creativity, or even for an understanding of it. Creativity is not consciously discouraged—indeed, lip service is always paid to it—but it often goes unrecognized. . . .

The bureaucratization of our society reflects not only a growing specialization but also deep-seated philosophical attitudes all the more pervasive for rarely being made explicit. Two generations of Americans have been shaped by the pragmatic conviction that inadequate performance is somehow the result of a failure to understand an "objective" environment properly and that group effort is valuable in itself. . . .

The result is a greater concern with the collection of facts than with an interpretation of their significance. . . .

The problem is magnified by the personal humility which is one of the most attractive American traits. Most Americans are convinced that no one is ever entirely "right," or, as the saying goes, that if there is disagreement each party is probably a little in error. The fear of dogmatism pervades the American scene. But the corollary of the tentativeness of most views is an incurable inner insecurity. Even very eminent people are reluctant to stand alone. Torn between the desire to be bold and the wish to be popular, they would like to see their boldness certified, as it were, by general approbation. Philosophical conviction and psychological bias thus combine to produce in and out of government a penchant for policymaking by committee. The obvious insurance against the possibility of error is to obtain as many opinions as possible. And unanimity is important, in that its absence is a standing reminder of the tentativeness of the course adopted. The committee approach to decision making is often less an organizational device than a spiritual necessity.

This is not to say, of course, that committees are inherently pernicious or that policy should be conducted on the basis of personal intuition. Most contemporary problems are so complex that the interaction of several minds is necessary for a full consideration. Any attempt to conduct policy on a personal basis inhibits creative approaches just as surely as does the purely administrative approach— witness the conduct of foreign policy by Secretary Dulles, whose technical virtuosity could not obscure the underlying stagnation.

The difficulty is not the existence of the committee system but the lengths to which reliance on it is pushed because of the lack of substantive mastery by the highest officials. . . .

. . . A policy dilemma indicates that the advantages and disadvantages of alternative measures appear fairly evenly balanced. . . . But in assessing these alternatives the risks always seem more certain than the opportunities. No one can ever prove that an opportunity existed, but failure to foresee a danger involves swift retribution. As a result, much of the committee procedure is designed to permit each participant or agency to register objections, and the system stresses avoidance of risk rather than boldness of conception. . . .

The attitudes of our high officials and their method of arriving at decisions inevitably distort the essence of policy. Effective policy depends not only on the skill of individual moves, but even more importantly on their relationship to each other. It requires a sense of proportion and a sense of style. All these intangibles are negated when problems become isolated cases, each of which is disposed of on its merits by experts or agencies in the special difficulties it involves. It is as if, in commissioning a painting, a patron would ask one artist to draw the face, another the body, another the hands, and still another the feet, simply because each artist was particularly good in one category. Such a procedure of stressing the components would sacrifice the meaning of the whole. . . .

The result is a vicious circle: As long as our high officials lack a framework of purpose, each problem becomes a special case. But the more fragmented the approach to policy becomes the more difficult it is to act consistently and purposefully. The typical pattern of our governmental process is therefore endless debate about whether a given set of circumstances is in fact a problem, until a crisis removes all doubts but also the possibility of effective action. The committee system, which is an attempt to reduce the inner insecurity of our top personnel, has the paradoxical consequence of institutionalizing it. . . .

The combination of unreflectiveness produced by the style of life of our most eminent people in and out of government, faith in administrative processes, and the conversational approach to policy has accounted for much of the uncertainty of our policy. It has led to an enormous waste of intellectual resources. The price we have paid for the absence of a sense of direction is that we have appeared to the rest of the world as vacillating, confused, and sometimes irrelevant.

It is sometimes argued that the characteristics described here are inseparable from the democratic process. But it surely is not inherent in a democracy that its most eminent people are formed by an experience which positively discourages political thinking and perhaps reflectiveness of any kind. . . .

... If our ablest people cannot be brought to address themselves to problems of national policy throughout their lives, no organizational device will save them from mediocrity once they reach high office. Substantial policy cannot be improvised. A democracy cannot function without a leadership group which has assurance in relation to the issues confronting it. We face, in short, a test of attitudes even more than of policies.

The Necessity for Choice, pp. 340-348.

One problem is the demand for expertise itself. Every problem which our society becomes concerned about—leaving aside the question of whether these are always the most significant—calls into being panels, committees, or study groups supported by either private or governmental funds. Many organizations constantly call on intellectuals for advice. As a result, intellectuals with a reputation soon find themselves so burdened that their pace of life hardly differs from that of the executives whom they counsel. They cannot supply perspective because they are as harassed as the policy makers. All pressures on them tend to keep them at the level of the performance which gained them their reputation. In his desire to be helpful, the intellectual is too frequently compelled to sacrifice what should be his greatest contribution to society—his creativity. . . .

The contribution of the intellectual to policy is therefore in terms of criteria that he has played only a minor role in establishing. He is rarely given the opportunity to point out that a query limits a range of possible solutions or that an issue is posed in irrelevant terms. He is asked to solve problems, not to contribute to the definition of goals. Where decisions are arrived at by negotiation, the intellectual—particularly if he is not himself part of the bureaucracy—is a useful weight in the scale. He can serve as a means of filtering ideas to the top outside of organizational channels or as one who legitimizes the viewpoint of contending factions within and among departments. This is why many organizations build up batteries of outside experts or create semi-independent research groups, and why articles or books become tools in the bureaucratic struggle. In short, all too often what the policymaker wants from the intellectual is not ideas but endorsement. . . .

Thus, if the intellectual is to make a contribution to national policy, he faces a delicate task. He must steer between the Scylla of letting the bureaucracy prescribe what is relevant or useful and the Charybdis of defining these criteria too abstractly. If he inclines too much toward the former, he will turn into a promoter of technical remedies; if he chooses the latter, he will run the risks of confusing dogmatism with morality and of courting martyrdom—of becoming, in short, as wrapped up in a cult of rejection as the activist is in a cult of success.

Where to draw the line between excessive commitment to the bureaucracy and paralyzing aloofness depends on so many intangibles of circumstance and personality that it is difficult to generalize. Perhaps the matter can be stated as follows: one of the challenges of the contemporary situation is to demonstrate the overwhelming importance of purpose over technique. The intellectual should therefore not refuse to participate in policymaking, for to do so confirms the stagnation of societies whose leadership groups have little substantive knowledge. But in co-operating the intellectual has two loyalties: to the organization that employs him and to values which transcend the bureaucratic framework and provide his basic motivation. . . .

Such an attitude requires an occasional separation from administration. The intellectual must guard his distinctive and, in this particular context, most crucial qualities: the pursuit of knowledge rather than of administrative ends and the perspective supplied by a non-bureaucratic vantage point. It is therefore essential for him to return from time to time to his library or his laboratory to "recharge his batteries." If he fails to do this, he will turn into an administrator, distinguished from some of his colleagues only by having been recruited from the intellectual community. Such a relationship does not preclude a major contribution. But it will then have to be in terms of the organization's criteria, which can be changed from within only by those in the most pre-eminent positions.

The Necessity for Choice, pp. 348-354.

. . . As long as our executives conceive their special skill to be a kind of intuitive ability to choose among conflicting advice on the basis of administrative or psychological criteria, our policy will be without a sense of proportion and a feeling for nuance. As long as our eminent men lack a substantive grasp of the issues, they will be unable to develop long-range policy or act with subtlety and assurance in the face of our challenges. . . .

The top leadership faces no more urgent responsibility than to combat the trends inherent in any highly elaborated society towards substituting routine for conception. The greater the seeming achievement, the heavier this duty. For the tragic aspect of history is that creativity is constantly in danger of being destroyed by success. The more effectively the environment is mastered, the greater is the temptation to rest on one's oars. The more an organization is elaborated, the easier it becomes to act by rote. Stagnation can then appear as well-being and blandness as wisdom. This is why creativity is usually at its height when society is sufficiently elaborate to keep choices from being random but the structure is not yet so overwhelming that the response verges on the mechanical. A society, if it is to remain vital, must be forever alert lest it confuse creativity with projecting the familiar into the future. . . .

The issue may therefore turn on a philosophical problem described earlier. The overemphasis on "realism" and the definition of "reality" as being entirely outside the observer may produce a certain passivity and a tendency to adapt to circumstance rather than to master it. It may also produce a gross underestimation of the ability to change, indeed to create, reality. To recapture the ability and the willingness to build our own reality is perhaps our ultimate challenge.

The Necessity for Choice, pp. 354, 356-357.

In the life of societies and international systems there comes a time when the question arises whether all the possibilities of innovation inherent in a given structure have been exhausted. At this point, symptoms are taken for causes; immediate problems absorb the attention that should be devoted to determining their significance. Events are not shaped by a concept of the future; the present becomes all-intrusive. However impressive such a structure may still appear to outsiders, it has passed its zenith. It will grow ever more rigid and, in time, irrelevant.

The West today confronts such a challenge. It has had centuries of "great" achievements punctuated by catastrophic upheaval. Its propensity for disaster has been high; but heretofore each tragedy was followed by a new burst of creativity. Are the stresses of today a sign of consolidation or the first symptoms of decay? Will they lead to renewal or to disintegration?

. . . Its challenge now is whether it can move from the nation-state to a larger community and draw from this effort the strength for another period of innovation.

The Troubled Partnership, p. 249.

The deepest question before the West may thus be what kind of vision it has of its future. With the growth of bureaucracy and expertise on both sides of the Atlantic, there is a danger of becoming mired by the prudent, the tactical or the expedient. Problems that are recognized are treated with considerable adeptness. But many problems are not recognized. The solution of immediate issues has priority over the shaping of the future. The expert has a vested interest in the existing framework; doing the familiar very well has, after all, made him an expert. His weakness is that he may confuse creativity with a projection of the present into the future. He respects "facts" and considers them something to be adjusted to, perhaps to be manipulated, but not to be transcended.

In the decades ahead, the West will have to lift its sights. When technique becomes exalted over purpose, men become the victims of their complexities. They forget that every great achievement in every field was a vision before it became a reality. Both sides of the Atlantic would do well to keep in mind that there are two kinds of realists: those who use facts and those who create them. The West requires nothing so much as men able to create their own reality.

The Troubled Partnership, p. 251.

This cynicism as to method has given rise to the argument that Bismarck was above all an opportunist. The charge of opportunism, however, begs the key issue of statesmanship. Anyone wishing to affect events must be opportunist to some extent. The real distinction is between those who adapt their purposes to reality and those who seek to mold reality in the light of their purposes.

"The White Revolutionary: Reflections on
Bismarck," pp. 909-910.

Facts can only be used—this was the motto of the new diplomacy which sought to keep the situation fluid through the dexterity of its manipulations until a constellation emerged reflecting the realities of power rather than the canons of legitimacy. Such a policy required cool nerves because it sought its objectives by the calm acceptance of great risks, of isolation, or of a sudden settlement at Prussia's expense. Its rewards were equally great—the emergence of a united Germany led by Prussia.

"The White Revolutionary: Reflections on
Bismarck," p. 213.

Something like [the purchase of certainty at the cost of creativity] seems to be characteristic of modern bureaucratic states whatever their ideology. In societies with a pragmatic tradition, such as the United States, there develops a greater concern with an analysis of where one is than where one is going. What passes for planning is frequently the projection of the familiar into the future. In societies based on ideology, doctrine is institutionalized and exegesis takes the place of innovation. Creativity must make so many concessions to orthodoxy that it may exhaust itself in doctrinal adaptations. In short, the accumulation of knowledge of the bureaucracy and the impersonality of its method of arriving at decisions can be achieved at a high price. Decision-making can grow so complex that the process of producing a bureaucratic consensus may overshadow the purpose of the effort. . . .

All of this drives the executive in the direction of extra-bureaucratic means of decision. The practice of relying on special emissaries or personal envoys is an example; their status outside the bureaucracy frees them from some of its restraints. International agreements are sometimes possible only by ignoring safeguards against capricious action. It is a paradoxical aspect of modern bureaucracies that their quest for objectivity and calculability often leads to impasses which can be overcome only by essentially arbitrary decisions.

American Foreign Policy, pp. 18-19, 23.

The collapse of the essentially aristocratic conception of foreign policy of the nineteenth century has made the career experiences of leaders even more crucial. An aristocracy—if it lives up to its values —will reject the arbitrariness of absolutist rule; and it will base itself on a notion of quality which discourages the temptations of demagoguery inherent in plebiscitarian democracy. Where position is felt to be a birthright, generosity is possible (though not guaranteed); flexibility is not inhibited by a commitment to perpetual success. Where a leader's estimate of himself is not completely dependent on his standing in an administrative structure, measures can be judged in terms of a conception of the future rather than of an almost compulsive desire to avoid even a temporary setback. When statesmen belonged to a community transcending national boundaries, there tended to be consensus on the criteria of what constituted a reasonable proposal. This did not prevent conflicts, but it did define their nature and encourage dialogue. The bane of aristocratic foreign policy was the risk of frivolousness, of a self-confidence unrelated to knowledge, and of too much emphasis on intuition.

In any event, ours is the age of the expert or the charismatic leader. The expert has his constituency—those who have a vested interest in commonly held opinions; elaborating and defining its consensus at a high level has, after all, made him an expert. Since the expert is often the product of the administrative dilemmas described earlier, he is usually in a poor position to transcend them. The charismatic leader, on the other hand, needs a perpetual revolution to maintain his position. Neither the expert nor the charismatic leader operates in an environment which puts a premium on long-range conceptions or on generosity or on subordinating the leader's ego to purposes which transcend his own career.

American Foreign Policy, pp. 28-29.

. . . . The main example of [bureaucratic-pragmatic] leadership is the American élite—though the leadership groups of other Western countries increasingly approximate the American pattern. Shaped by a society without fundamental social schisms (at least until the race problem became visible) and the product of an environment in which most recognized problems have proved soluble, its approach to policy is *ad hoc*, pragmatic, and somewhat mechanical. . . .

This is reinforced by the special qualities of the professions—law and business—which furnish the core of the leadership groups in America. Lawyers—at least in the Anglo-Saxon tradition—prefer to deal with actual rather than hypothetical cases; they have little confidence in the possibility of stating a future issue abstractly. . . .

The attitudes of the business élite reinforce the convictions of the legal profession. The American business executive rises through a process of selection which rewards the ability to manipulate the known—in itself a conciliatory procedure. . . .

All this gives American policy its particular cast. Problems are dealt with as they arise. Agreement on what constitutes a problem generally depends on an emerging crisis which settles the previously inconclusive disputes about priorities. When a problem is recognized, it is dealt with by mobilization of all resources to overcome the immediate symptoms. This often involves the risk of slighting longer-term issues which may not yet have assumed crisis proportions and of overwhelming, perhaps even undermining, the structure of the area concerned by a flood of American technical experts proposing remedies on an American scale. Administrative decisions emerge from a compromise of conflicting pressures in which accidents of personality or persuasiveness play a crucial role. The compromise often reflects the maxim that "if two parties disagree the truth is usually somewhere in between." But the pedantic application of such truisms causes the various contenders to exaggerate their positions for bargaining purposes or to construct fictitious extremes to make their position appear moderate. In either case, internal bargaining predominates over substance. . . .

104

. . . In short, the American leadership groups show high competence in dealing with technical issues, and much less virtuosity in mastering a historical process. And the policies of other Western countries exhibit variations of the American pattern. A lesser pragmatism in continental Europe is counterbalanced by a smaller ability to play a world-role.

American Foreign Policy, pp. 29, 30, 32-34.

The statesman manipulates reality; his first goal is survival; he feels responsible not only for the best but also for the worst conceivable outcome. His view of human nature is wary; he is conscious of many great hopes which have failed, of many good intentions that could not be realized, of selfishness and ambition and violence. He is, therefore, inclined to erect hedges against the possibility that even the most brilliant idea might prove abortive and that the most eloquent formulation might hide ulterior motives. He will try to avoid certain experiments, not because he would object to the results if they succeeded, but because he would feel himself responsible for the consequences if they failed. He is suspicious of those who personalize foreign policy, for history teaches him the fragility of structures dependent on individuals. To the statesman, gradualism is the essence of stability; he represents an era of average performance, of gradual change and slow construction.

By contrast, the prophet is less concerned with manipulating than with creating reality. What is possible interests him less than what is "right." He offers his vision as the test and his good faith as a guarantee. He believes in total solutions; he is less absorbed in methodology than in purpose. He believes in the perfectibility of man. His approach is timeless and not dependent on circumstances. He objects to gradualism as an unnecessary concession to circumstance. He will risk everything because his vision is the primary significant reality to him. Paradoxically, his more optimistic view of human nature makes him more intolerant than the statesman. If truth is both knowable and attainable, only immorality or stupidity can keep man from realizing it. The prophet represents an era of exaltation, of great upheavals, of vast accomplishments, but also of enormous disasters.

The encounter between the political and the prophetic approach to policy is always somewhat inconclusive and frustrating. The test of the statesman is the permanence of the international structure under stress. The test of the prophet is inherent in his vision. The statesman will seek to reduce the prophet's intuition to precise measures; he judges ideas on their utility and not on their "truth." To the prophet this approach is almost sacrilegious because it represents the triumph of expediency over universal principles. To the statesman negotiation is the mechanism of stability because it presupposes that maintenance of the existing order is more important than any dispute within it. To the prophet negotiations can have only symbolic value—as a means of converting or demoralizing the opponent; truth, by definition, cannot be compromised.

Both approaches have prevailed at different periods in history. The political approach dominated European foreign policy between the end of the religious wars and the French Revolution and then again between the Congress of Vienna and the outbreak of World War I. The prophetic mode was in the ascendant during the great upheavals of the religious struggles and the period of the French Revolution, and in the contemporary uprisings in major parts of the world.

American Foreign Policy, pp. 46-48.

The dilemma is that there can be no stability without equilibrium but, equally, equilibrium is not a purpose with which we can respond to the travail of our world. A sense of mission is clearly a legacy of American history; to most Americans, America has always stood for something other than its own grandeur. But a clearer understanding of America's interests and of the requirements of equilibrium can give perspective to our idealism and lead to humane and moderate objectives, especially in relation to political and social change. Thus our conception of world order must have deeper purposes than stability but greater restraints on our behavior than would result if it were approached only in a fit of enthusiasm.

American Foreign Policy, p. 94.

The prerequisite for a fruitful national debate is that the policymakers and critics appreciate each other's perspectives and respect each other's purposes. The policymaker must understand that the critic is obliged to stress imperfections in order to challenge assumptions and to goad actions. But equally the critic should acknowledge the complexity and inherent ambiguity of the policymaker's choices. The policymaker must be concerned with the best that can be achieved, not just the best that can be imagined. He has to act in a fog of incomplete knowledge without the information that will be available later to the analyst. He knows—or should know—that he is responsible for the consequences of disaster as well as for the benefits of success. He may have to qualify some goals, not because they would be undesirable if reached but because the risks of failure outweigh potential gains. He must often settle for the gradual, much as he might prefer the immediate. He must compromise with others, and this means to some extent compromising with himself.

The outsider demonstrates his morality by the precision of his perceptions and the loftiness of his ideals. The policymaker expresses his morality by implementing a sequence of imperfections and partial solutions in pursuit of *his* ideals.

There must be understanding, as well, of the crucial importance of timing. Opportunities cannot be hoarded; once past, they are usually irretrievable. New relationships in a fluid transitional period —such as today—are delicate and vulnerable; they must be nurtured if they are to thrive. We cannot pull up young shoots periodically to see whether the roots are still there or whether there is some marginally better location for them.

Pacem in Terris Speech, p. 527.

LIST OF REFERENCES

Conquest, Robert, et al. "Detente: An Evaluation." *Survey*, Spring-Summer 1974.

Draper, Theodore. "Detente." *Commentary*, June 1974.

Grossman, Gregory. Statement before the Joint Economic Committee. In *Hearings on the Soviet Economic Outlook*, 93rd Congress, 1st session, July 17–19, 1973.

Kissinger, Henry A. *American Foreign Policy, Three Essays.* New York: W. W. Norton, 1969.

————. "American Policy and Preventive War." *Yale Review*, vol. 44, no. 3 (April 1955).

————. "Limitations of Diplomacy." *New Republic*, May 6, 1955.

————. "Limited War: Nuclear or Conventional? A Reappraisal." *Daedalus*, Fall 1960.

————. *The Necessity for Choice: Prospects of American Foreign Policy.* New York: Harper and Row, 1961.

————. *Nuclear Weapons and Foreign Policy.* New York: Harper and Brothers, for the Council on Foreign Relations, 1957.

————. "The Price of German Unity." *The Reporter*, April 22, 1965.

————. "Reflections on American Diplomacy." *Foreign Affairs*, October 1956.

————. "The Search for Stability." *Foreign Affairs*, July 1959.

————. Speech in Minneapolis. *Department of State Bulletin*, August 4, 1975.

————. Speech to the American Legion. *Department of State Bulletin*, September 16, 1974.

————. Speech to the Pilgrims of Great Britain. *Department of State Bulletin*, December 31, 1973.

———. Speech to the Third Pacem in Terris Conference. *Department of State Bulletin,* October 29, 1973.

———. Speech to the UN General Assembly. *Department of State Press Release,* no. 496 (September 22, 1975).

———. Statement to the Senate Finance Committee. *Department of State Bulletin,* April 1, 1974.

———. Statement to the Senate Foreign Relations Committee. *Department of State Bulletin,* October 14, 1974.

———. *The Troubled Partnership: A Reappraisal of the Atlantic Alliance.* New York: McGraw-Hill, 1965.

———. "The White Revolutionary: Reflections on Bismarck." *Daedalus,* Summer 1968.

———. *A World Restored: Castlereagh, Metternich and Restoration of Peace, 1812–1822.* Boston: Houghton-Mifflin, 1957.

Solzhenitsyn, Alexander. Speech delivered in Washington. Reported in *U.S. News and World Report,* July 14, 1975.

U.S. Congress. Senate Armed Services Committee. Statement of the chairman, Joint Chiefs of Staff, on United States Military Posture for FY1975. In *Hearings on S. 300,* 93rd Congress, 2d session, February 5, 1974.

U.S. Department of Defense. *Annual Defense Report: FY1976 and FY197T.* Washington, D. C.: U.S. Government Printing Office, 1975.

U.S. Foreign Policy for the 1970's: Shaping a Durable Peace. A Report to the Congress by Richard Nixon, President of the United States. Washington, D. C.: U.S. Government Printing Office, 1973.

Voss, Earl. "Defending Europe with Blunderbusses." Reprint 24. Washington, D. C.: American Enterprise Institute, 1974.

Wohlstetter, Albert. "Threats and Promises of Peace: Europe and America in the New Era." *Orbis,* Winter 1974.

ACKNOWLEDGMENTS

Grateful acknowledgment is made to the following publishers for their permissions to reprint excerpts from the books and articles of Henry A. Kissinger listed below.

The Necessity for Choice: Prospects of American Foreign Policy. © 1960, 1961 by Henry A. Kissinger; used with permission of Harper & Row, Publishers, Inc.

Nuclear Weapons and Foreign Policy. Used with permission of the Council on Foreign Relations, Inc.

The Troubled Partnership: A Reappraisal of the Atlantic Alliance. © 1965 by the Council on Foreign Relations, Inc.; used with permission of McGraw-Hill Book Company.

A World Restored: Castlereagh, Metternich and Restoration of Peace, 1812-1922. Used with permission of Houghton-Mifflin Company.

American Foreign Policy, Three Essays. © 1968 by the Brookings Institution; © 1969, 1974 by Henry A. Kissinger; used with permission of W. W. Norton & Company, Inc.

"The Price of German Unity." © 1965 by The Reporter Magazine Company.

"The White Revolutionary: Reflections on Bismarck." Used with permission of *Daedalus*, Journal of the American Academy of Arts and Sciences.

"American Policy and Preventive War." Used with permission of *The Yale Review.*

"Limitations of Diplomacy." © 1955 by The New Republic, Inc.

"Reflections on American Diplomacy" and "The Search for Stability." *Foreign Affairs.* © 1956, 1959 by the Council on Foreign Relations, Inc.

Cover and book design: Pat Taylor